P9-CAS-758

TREATING PATIENTS
WITH NEUROPSYCHOLOGICAL
DISORDERS

Psychologists in Independent Practice

Michael J. Murphy, Series Editor

TREATING PATIENTS WITH NEUROPSYCHOLOGICAL DISORDERS: A CLINICIAN'S GUIDE TO ASSESSMENT AND REFERRAL

JEFFERY B. ALLEN

AMERICAN PSYCHOLOGICAL ASSOCIATION

WASHINGTON, DC

Copyright © 2002 by the American Psychological Association. All rights
reserved. Except as permitted under the United States Copyright Act of
1976, no part of this publication may be reproduced or distributed in any
form or by any means, or stored in a database or retrieval system, without
the prior written permission of the publisher.

Published by
American Psychological Association
750 First Street, NE
Washington, DC 20002
www.apa.org

To order	Tel: (800) 374-2721, Direct: (202) 336-5510
APA Order Department	Fax: (202) 336-5502, TDD/TTY: (202) 336-6123
P.O. Box 92984	Online: www.apa.org/books/
Washington, DC 20090-2984	Email: order@apa.org

In the U.K., Europe, Africa, and the Middle East, copies may be ordered from
American Psychological Association
3 Henrietta Street
Covent Garden, London
WC2E 8LU England

Typeset in Palatino by EPS Group Inc., Easton, MD

Printer: Goodway Graphics, Springfield, VA
Cover designer: Minker Design, Bethesda, MD
Technical/Production Editor: Jennifer Powers

The opinions and statements published are the responsibility of the authors,
and such opinions and statements do not necessarily represent the policies of
the American Psychological Association.

Library of Congress Cataloging-in-Publication Data
Allen, Jeffery B.
    Treating patients with neuropsychological disorders : a clinician's guide
to assessment and referral / Jeffery B. Allen.
        p.   cm.—(Psychologists in independent practice)
    Includes bibliographical references and index.
    ISBN 1-55798-825-0 (softcover : alk. paper)
        1. Clinical neuropsychology.   2. Neurobehavioral disorders—
Patients.   3. Neuropsychiatry.   I. Psychologists in independent practice
book series

    RC341. A43   2001
    616.8—dc21

                                                                    2001022857

British Library Cataloguing-in-Publication Data
A CIP record is available from the British Library.

Printed in the United States of America
First Edition

Contents

Acknowledgments

Many of my friends and colleagues contributed to the impetus for the development of this book. They include James Heck, Mark A. Williams, and Mark Aloia. I am also grateful to Leon VandeCreek, Robert Rando, and Brian Thomas for their thoughtful review of the manuscript and extended discussions concerning ways to improve the readability of the text. My wife, Debbie Allen, helped me in countless ways with her editorial expertise, ability to clarify my thoughts, and unwavering support through the trials of writing a book. The project would not have been possible without her. Finally, I would like to dedicate this book to my parents, James and Marilyn Allen, who continue to inspire and support me.

TREATING PATIENTS
WITH NEUROPSYCHOLOGICAL
DISORDERS

Introduction

General practitioners are often the first to encounter clients who have not only psychological disorders but also medical disorders. A conservative assumption is that at least 10% of patients seen by general practitioners also have a causative or contributing organic disease (Taylor, 1990). Koran et al. (1989) found that approximately 12% of clients seen in the mental health system had comorbid physical illness that was unrecognized at the intake evaluation, and 17% of these individuals had organic conditions that either caused or exacerbated the psychological symptoms for which they were being treated. Neurological problems commonly mistaken for psychological disorders include toxic metabolic conditions that affect the brain, temporal lobe epilepsy, brain tumors, and multi-infarct dementia. Failing to identify and appropriately treat such physical or neurological problems can place patients at risk of further psychological decline, serious medical complications, or death. When epilepsy, for example, is misdiagnosed as paranoid schizophrenia and therefore not treated correctly, the condition can result in cumulative cognitive neurological decline, loss of function, and premature death.

The emergent understanding that neuropsychological impairment is a common comorbidity for many general-practice clients is just one reason the general clinician must refine his or her awareness of what to do when he or she encounters such clients. Increasingly definitive guidelines for training and practice in the field of clinical neuropsychology also affect today's general clinician, in two related and significant ways. No longer does the general clinician's background meet established requirements for performing neuropsychological services. Now more than ever, however, general clinicians can rely on the assistance of individuals highly trained in this area of concentration. In addition, recent developments and increasing sophistication in the detection of neuropsychological problems can provide general practitioners with assessment tools previously unavailable.

Mindful of the specialized nature of neuropsychological services, psychologists working in general-practice arenas often express a need for additional information about how to screen for neuropsychological, or cognitive, impairment; when to refer for comprehensive neuropsychological evaluation; how to assist with a referral to a neuropsychologist; and how to use information from the neuropsychological report to facilitate ongoing clinical work with a client. This book is a direct response to that need. Many existing textbooks, clearly intended for the specialist in clinical neuropsychology, exhaustively cover neuropsychological disorders and their comprehensive cognitive assessment. Other offerings deal with only the issue of screening for neuropsychological impairment. They cover the frequently unidimensional task of administering screening tests to classify patients in a binary manner as either "brain-damaged" or "normal." These textbooks include, in encyclopedic fashion, only tests believed to serve screening functions. They do not methodically and thoughtfully provide the general practitioner with a comprehensive road map for navigating the complexities that accompany clinical work with clients who have cognitive impairment.

Filling a portion of this expressed void, this book may be used as a reference when the issue of neuropsychological status is clinically relevant. It details pertinent intake and patient history factors, signs and symptoms indicative of possible neuropsychological issues, indicators within frequently administered psychological tests that can alert the clinician to the potential of cognitive impairment, and issues surrounding the use of screening measures. It also provides information about when to make a referral to a clinical neuropsychologist, how to effectively manage such a referral, and how to use information generated by the referral.

Given the scope of this textbook as a reference for the generalist using specialized services in neuropsychology, space does not permit an exhaustive treatment of all topics noted. For this reason, each chapter in the book includes a section titled *Additional Readings* that provides supplemental coverage of these critical topics. These cogent and useful sources on topics within the field of clinical neuropsychology include more detailed information regarding neuroanatomy and neuropathology, specific neurological illness and accompanying neurobehavioral syndromes, approaches to neuropsychological assessment, and issues related to treating clients with neurobehavioral deficits. These references were selected because of their quality, utility, and reputation within the discipline.

Three groups of practitioners will find this text helpful. The majority of general practitioners engaged in psychotherapeutic-based practices—clinicians who typically do not deal with the uniquely challenging population of neurologically impaired clients but desire assistance in obtaining neuropsychological services for such clients—will find information about referring clients to a clinical neuropsychologist. General practitioners who encounter and seek to treat clients with possible cognitive impairment may use the book for suggestions on tailoring treatment plans to meet individual clients' needs. Clinicians who conduct general assessments and are often required to comment on the developmental (vs. acquired) etiology of observed cognitive deficits—a charge that is outside the academic and training background of many general practitioners—also may benefit from data provided in the book. Along with currently practicing clinicians, this book also is well suited for graduate students and individuals training to provide general clinical services.

This book is not intended as an alternative to formal training in clinical neuropsychology as outlined by the International Neuropsychology Society and Division 40 (Clinical Neuropsychology) of the American Psychological Association (APA). As with many specialties in psychology, clinical neuropsychology continues to be defined by increasingly specific guidelines for appropriate training. Hess and Hart (1990) asserted that neuropsychological evaluations should be administered and interpreted by only those individuals who have requisite training and experience. The Houston Conference on Specialty Education and Training in Clinical Neuropsychology (Hannay et al., 1998) resulted in clear descriptions of the didactic and practical experiences that should precede specialty practice in the field. A summary of the Houston conference can be obtained from APA's Division 40, the International Neuropsychology Society, or the National Academy of Neuropsychology. Finally, the "Ethical Principles of Psychologists and Code of Conduct" (APA, 1992) should be consulted when clinicians have questions regarding the scope of their professional practice or competency. Thus, this book is not intended to exhaustively cover the field of clinical neuropsychology and is not a how-to manual for performing comprehensive neuropsychological assessment.

Overview

Part I of the text (chapters 1 and 2) provides an introduction to clinical neuropsychology and related fields and technical information that is fundamental to building a knowledge base one can tap when faced with neuropsychologically involved clients. Chapter 1 reviews the spectrum of services surrounding neuropsychological impairment and describes professionals involved in the evaluation and management of patients who have sustained neurological compromise. Detailed descriptions of neuropsychology, the rehabilitation professions (physical therapy, occupational therapy, speech and language therapy, and recreational therapy), and vocational rehabilitation counseling are provided. The allied professions of physical medicine, neurology and its affiliated laboratory techniques, psychiatry, and social work also are described. Chapter 2 provides a review of, or introduction to, basic functional neuroanatomy from a neuropsychological perspective, with an emphasis on clinical relevance. The chapter describes functional contributions of neural structures within the central nervous system. Aspects of Luria's conceptualization of brain–behavior relations are discussed within an overarching description of brain function. Supportive systems that serve critical maintenance functions for the central nervous system are also discussed.

Part II (chapters 3–5) provides an overview of neurological and developmental conditions that can produce cognitive or psychological changes. It also presents clinical strategies to assist in detecting such conditions and making appropriate referrals. Chapter 3 provides synopses of various neurological disorders, including head trauma; vascular disease; dementia; epilepsy; neoplasm; and infectious, metabolic, and endocrine conditions. Along with information about the neurobehavioral consequences of neurological disorders, basic material concerning medical presentation, symptomatology, and treatment approaches is included to assist the clinician in communicating with physicians and other professionals who are confronted more routinely with these issues. Chapter 4 explores the neuropsychological consequences of nonneurological conditions and psychosocial factors. Because psychological states such as depression, anxiety, and somatization can affect neuropsychological test performance, the general clinician should be aware of how psychological conditions can lead to particular patterns of cognitive decline. Chapter 5 deals with indicators of neuropsychological dysfunction, including information obtained during the clinical interview and found in the medical record, qualitative aspects of behaviors, and indications found on common psychological measures. The chapter also provides suggestions and guidelines for supplementary testing that can elucidate a client's neuropsychological difficulties. Chapter 5 also educates the clinician on obtaining clinical information that can facilitate subsequent referrals to neuropsychologists, eliminating the redundancy that often accompanies such referrals.

Part III (chapters 6 and 7) focuses on relevant issues and practical strategies for effective referral for services in neuropsychology and related clinical disciplines. It also discusses the application of neuropsychological findings to case management and psychotherapeutic interventions with individuals demonstrating both general cognitive impairment and specific neurological populations, such as patients with cerebrovascular disease or brain tumors. Chapter 6 presents information and pragmatic suggestions regarding the referral process. General clinicians are often disappointed by the applicability of conclusions and recommendations that arise from the neuropsychological evaluation process. A systematic method of organizing referral questions and clinical needs enhances the usefulness of the neuropsychological report that is returned to the clinician. The chapter opens with suggestions for making effective referrals. It comprises an overview of the neuropsychological assessment process, the manner in which neuropsychological data are interpreted, and an outline of the neuropsychological report format. The chapter concludes with a discussion of follow-up with neuropsychology and additional testing related to psychosocial adjustment to be performed by the clinician who continues to provide therapy to the client.

Chapter 7 is concerned with case management and covers issues related to psychological intervention with cognitively involved clients. The focus is on using neuropsychological findings in treatment planning. A major area discussed is the issue of modifying the structure of psychological intervention when working with individuals with deficits in attention, memory, language, and other cognitive skills critical to the efficacy of psychological intervention. Themes that frequently arise in treating cognitively involved clients (e.g., awareness of deficits, feelings of loss) also are considered. Chapter 7 looks at specific neurological populations, such as head trauma, stroke, and brain tumor, and the myriad psychological and social issues that are critical to the adjustment of these individuals. The chapter also deals with relevant forms of group therapy.

Interested practitioners will further increase their knowledge by accessing the valuable information provided by the articles and texts recommended in the book's *Additional Reading* sections. Used continually as a reference and resource, this book will help the general clinician confidently and appropriately intervene with neurologically involved clients.

I

Neuropsychology Fundamentals

1

Clinical Neuropsychology and Allied Disciplines

Many general practitioners encounter *neurologically involved* clients, those who manifest symptoms of a neurological illness or injury. When this occurs, the general practitioner can refine treatment by utilizing the resources of a variety of allied disciplines. Clinical neuropsychologists are just one type of specialist who can provide insight and assistance regarding neurologically involved clients. Others are physiatrists, neurologists, psychiatrists, physical and occupational therapists, speech and language pathologists, recreational therapists, clinical social workers, and vocational rehabilitation counselors. General clinicians can obtain information from allied professionals with whom a client has already had contact, or he or she can refer to such professionals for assistance with the client.

In this chapter I provide information about background, training requirements, and facility placements for the newer or less familiar disciplines. Appendix A is a list of contact organizations that can provide more information about these fields.

Clinical Neuropsychology

Clinical neuropsychology involves the study of brain–behavior relations. To understand, assess, and provide treat-

11

ment for neuropsychological disorders, the field integrates the knowledge bases of behavioral neurology, classical neuroscience, and psychometric theory. Through the study of normal and damaged neural systems, clinical neuropsychologists attempt to understand disrupted functions in the domains of attention, learning, and memory; visuoperceptual abilities; language; and executive control (frontal lobe functions). They also are concerned with the impact of altered functioning on overarching human phenomena, such as self-awareness, emotional expression, and personality in general. In practical terms, clinical neuropsychologists focus on developing useful and reliable assessment strategies and effective means of intervention for these issues.

The typical neuropsychologist has obtained a PhD in clinical psychology, with an emphasis on coursework in brain–behavior relations and related practicum experiences. In addition, many neuropsychologists complete specialty internships and postdoctoral training that often take place in medical settings.

Clinical neuropsychologists practice in general hospitals and postacute rehabilitation hospitals. They also may be found in academic and community private practice settings.

Areas of Professional Focus Within Clinical Neuropsychology

Pediatric clinical neuropsychology. Child clinical neuropsychology involves the study of brain function and behavior in children and adolescents (Teeter & Semrud-Clikeman, 1997). This subdiscipline emerged from the disciplines of clinical neuroscience, developmental and cognitive psychology, pediatric neurology, adult neuropsychology, and school psychology (Batchelor & Dean, 1996; Williams & Boll, 1997). Child clinical neuropsychology has progressed through several stages during its development over the past 30–40 years (Tramontana & Hooper, 1988) and is currently in a stage Rourke (1982) termed the *dynamic phase*, with a focus on ecological validity of neuropsychological assessment procedures. This phase is accompanied by declining emphasis on diagnosing brain impairment and increasing interest in providing a comprehensive functional assessment of the child from a biopsychosocial framework. This comprehensive focus lends itself more fully to purposes of treatment and management (Williams & Boll, 1997).

Although the application of neuropsychological principles to the study of children has advantages for clinical assessment and intervention, the subdiscipline also carries some unique challenges. For example, brain organization in children is poorly understood (Batchelor & Dean, 1996, Hynd & Willis, 1988). Also, the dynamic nature of neurological and cognitive development in children results in rapidly changing expectations of what is typical on a battery of neuropsychological tests. Unlike the static nature of neuropsychological functioning in adult patients, premorbid stability cannot be assumed in children. The brain's plasticity and reorganizational capacity during certain periods of childhood also complicate the neuropsychologist's task of identifying areas of impairment following traumatic insult. Moreover, the child neuropsychologist encounters a different mix of clinical cases than that seen by a neuropsychologist who sees primarily adults. Child clinicians see a greater proportion of developmentally related conditions, such as learning disabilities, attention deficit disorders, and autism.

On the other hand, unique opportunities exist for a child neuropsychologist to meaningfully intervene with a child manifesting cognitive or behavioral deficits. A child's greater degree of neurodevelopmental flexibility offers more extensive potential for remediation or compensatory interventions. In addition, child neuropsychologists seem to have more occasions to inform critical individuals (parents, teachers, etc.) of the implications of evaluation findings. In many cases, recommendations from a report are recapitulated at the beginning of each school year.

Geriatric clinical neuropsychology. As the number of individuals living beyond age 65 rises, so too does the incidence of dementia and cognitive impairment (Debettignles, Swihart, Green, & Pirozzolo, 1997). These increases have created the need for professionals trained to deal with the unique medical, psychological, and cognitive difficulties associated with growing older.

Neuropsychological assessment of older individuals has many meaningful clinical applications. First, in the face of the limited specificity of many medical diagnostic tests, neuropsychological testing represents one method of early detection for dementing illness. Second, specific cognitive deficits demonstrated on neuropsychological tests can supply information critical to differential diagnosis. Efficient detection and diagnosis of various disorders that affect older people can greatly facilitate medical intervention and management of such patients. Third, baseline and follow-up neuropsychological assessment can provide estimates of the severity and the speed of progression of various conditions. This information is helpful for case management, family intervention, and long-term planning for individuals who display chronic, progressive conditions, such as Alzheimer's disease, that require increasing levels of supervision, social support, and financial resources.

As with the child neuropsychologist, some unique challenges face the geriatric neuropsychologist. One factor that complicates interpretation of neuropsychological findings is the degree of comorbidity in elderly patients. It is not uncommon to assess individuals in whom multiple systemic, neurological, and psychiatric conditions affect neurobehavioral status. Apportioning impairments to each of the known conditions can be difficult or impossible yet may be the basis for the referral. A paucity of normative information regarding the performance of older individuals, particularly those older than 80, on neuropsychological tests creates another obstacle for the geriatric neuropsychologist. Related to the issue of available norms is the concept of what is considered "normal aging." Some practitioners compare a client's data with that of same-age individuals with no known medical, neurological, or psychological diagnosis, but others suggest that such "super-normals" represent a limited and uncharacteristic aspect of the geriatric population. A fourth consideration is cognitive or motor slowing that accompanies aging. This speed-of-response factor can affect performance on tests across several cognitive domains in a diffuse and superfluous manner that limits detailed or clinically meaningful interpretation.

The uniqueness of the applications and obstacles inherent to geriatric neuropsychology creates a demand for focused training and practice. The number of graduate and postdoctoral training experiences within the subspecialty of geriatric neuropsychology as well as relevant coverage in the neuropsychological literature have increased.

Physiatry

A physiatrist is a physician who specializes in physical medicine and rehabilitation (PM&R). PM&R deals with the diagnosis, treatment, and prevention of injuries and disorders that produce temporary or chronic impairment of function. It is concerned with restoration of function brought about by illness or injury that results in declines in mobility, self-care, and productivity or in reduced cognitive capacity.

The specialty evolved during the 1930s as a response to the treatment requirements of individuals who had neurological or musculoskeletal disorders. World War II rapidly expanded the need for a field of professionals prepared to deal with thousands of veterans who sustained disabilities that compromised their vocational capacities and independent functioning. At the time PM&R became a board-certified specialty in 1947, there were fewer than 100 board-certified physiatrists. Today, approximately 5,000 practitioners are board-certified physiatrists.

Physiatrists approach patients in a comprehensive fashion rather than in the reductionistic manner inherent to many medical specialties. In many cases, the physiatrist addresses and synthesizes medical, social, emotional, familial, and legal aspects of a patient's impairments. Consequently, many physiatrists lead multidisciplinary treatment teams that comprise psychologists, social workers, nurses, physical therapists, occupational therapists, and speech and language pathologists. Such interdisciplinary contexts are most relevant in the treatment of conditions that compromise the central nervous system (CNS), such as stroke, spinal cord injury, and traumatic brain injury (TBI). PM&R, perhaps more than any specialty, has become aligned with the "quality of life" concept that has emerged dramatically in the medical field during the last 3–5 years.

The physiatrist accesses laboratory diagnostic procedures, including electrodiagnostic techniques such as evoked potentials (electrical responses in the brain that follow sensory stimulation), nerve conduction studies, and electromyography. In general, these methods assist in identifying the source and magnitude of brain dysfunction that has resulted in paresis (muscle weakness), incoordination, spasticity, or pain. The armamentarium of the physiatrist in treating specific physical problems includes medication, therapeutic exercise, electrical stimulation of the local area of impairment, and assistive devices.

Although these measures usually suffice for patients with conditions that do not include cognitive or behavioral facets, patients with more involved disorders or disorders that affect the CNS require management of psychological or cognitive impairments. Some physiatrists, therefore, specialize in the treatment of patients who have sustained primarily cognitive or neurobehavioral impairments. In such cases, the physiatrist is often principally responsible for coordinating evaluation and treatment for their patients by requesting and integrating the services of neurologists, neuropsychologists, speech therapists, and psychologists.

Four years of graduate medical education followed by a 4-year postdoctoral residency are required to become a physiatrist. During residency, the physiatrist spends 1 year developing basic clinical skills and 3 years training in the specialty.

Physiatrists can be found in rehabilitation centers, acute-care hospitals, and outpatient settings. They may specialize in occupational medicine, pain management, or sports medicine.

Neurology

When the general clinician has clients whose impairments have neurological etiologies, the neurologist is a critical contributor to the consultation process. During the initial evaluation, a neurologist typically gathers a complete history of the presenting problem and conducts an extensive neurological examination that can require up to 60 min of contact with the patient. Following this initial assessment, the neurologist may request that the patient undergo additional neurodiagnostic procedures, such as an electroencephalogram (EEG), computerized tomography (CT), or magnetic resonance imaging (MRI).

A rudimentary understanding of basic methodology will assist general clinicians when interacting with neurologists, who emerge from a very different professional culture. Therefore, I now briefly describe the neurological examination and the neurodiagnostic procedures noted above.

Neurological Examination

A neurological examination results in a comprehensive clinical record of the patient's level of alertness and consciousness, sensory integrity, reflexes, movement and muscle tone, and basic cognitive responsiveness. Many times the exam begins with an appraisal of sensory functions as supported by the cranial nerves. Visual acuity, the breadth of the visual periphery, and pupillary response are investigated. Olfaction, audition, and tactile sense at various points on the body's surface also are tested. Three specific types of reflexes are tested. *Muscle stretch reflexes*, or *deep-tendon reflexes*, such as the patellar reflex, are tested by response to a swift strike in the area of the tendon. *Superficial reflexes* are elicited by lightly stroking the surface of the skin and observing contraction of the underlying muscle. *Pathologic reflexes*, or *release reflexes*, which are elicited by various methods, should not be found after infancy and so, if found, can be useful in diagnosing focal CNS disease. Motor examination includes assessment of balance and gait and clinical investigation of muscle bulk and strength, limb tone, and involuntary and voluntary movement. The exam usually concludes with a gross examination of attention and concentration, language, memory, visuospatial capacity, and abstract reasoning. An absence of deficits in these higher cognitive functions often triggers a referral for a more sensitive neuropsychological evaluation.

Electroencephalography

The EEG is one of neurology's most widely used investigative techniques. In this procedure, electrodes are placed systematically on the scalp to record the activity of the brain. Placement of the electrodes is standardized, and the electrical wave form activity of each pair of electrodes is recorded as an independent channel. A common method of placement is the 10–20 international system seen in Figure 1.1. The EEG can provide diagnostic assistance in detection and localization of brain lesions such as brain abscesses, tumors, or infarcts (areas of damaged tissue), but it is most effective in the evaluation of epileptic disorders—specifically, the abnormal

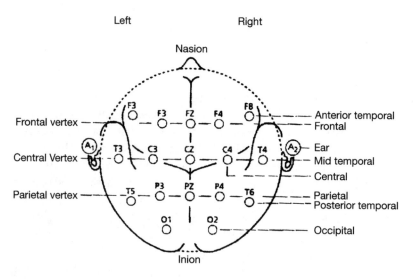

Figure 1.1. Electroencephalogram electrode placement using the 10–20 International Placement System.

electrical discharge that occurs during an *ictus* (seizure episode). Such wave form abnormalities may be apparent in several channels, or they may be confined to an area of the brain
that corresponds to a single channel (e.g., above the temporal
region; Walsh, 1994).

CT

In general, CT involves scanning a target body part, such as
the brain, with a focused beam of x-rays, permitting the
transmission of x-ray photons to the tissue that is to be measured for density. A series of standard "cuts," or scanning
passes, is generated at successive levels of the brain. The
quantitative data gleaned from these scans are processed by
a computer that produces a visual image of the brain. Neuropathology is marked by variations in normal density,
which are revealed by the degree of darkness on the film.
Mass effects—effects secondary to space-occupying brain pathology (e.g., tumor)—are visualized as displacement of
well-known neuroanatomic landmarks (e.g., pineal gland,
lateral ventricles).

MRI

Unlike CT, MRI does not require x-rays. Palmer (1985) provided a clear description of the basis for the MRI:

> When the nuclei of certain atoms—usually hydrogen
> protons—are placed in a high magnetic field, they align
> with the axis of spin in the direction of the field. A ra-
> diofrequency applied at right angles to the field changes
> the angle of spin, and the return to equilibrium when the
> radiofrequency pulse ceases is associated with the emis-
> sion of a radiofrequency characteristic of the element and
> its physiochemical environment. In MRI, gradient mag-
> netic fields in the three directions allow spatial detection
> of signal data and a two-dimensional image to be formed
> (p. 3).

Technology and the clinical literature base surrounding MRI has expanded at a rapid rate, and MRI is favored over the CT scan in many diagnostic contexts. It has been proposed that MRI eventually will replace CT as a method of visualizing the brain and diagnosing brain lesions (Franken et al., 1986). The MRI is superior in revealing evidence of tumors of the brain; however, CT may continue to be the method of choice when looking for the presence of calcification, skull fractures, or other bony abnormalities (Reitan & Wolfson, 1992).

Psychiatry

Many neurologically involved clients have accompanying emotional or psychological disturbance that requires psychiatric services for diagnosis, medication, or long-term management. Patients may be referred for psychiatric assessment in a variety of situations. First, neurologically impaired patients may possess emotional difficulties that predate the neurological diagnosis. For example, individuals with TBI may possess premorbid personality characteristics (e.g., risk taking, impulsivity) that lead to a high potential for neurological accidents. Second, certain injuries to or illnesses of the brain produce predictable psychiatric syndromes. For example, damage to the orbital frontal region of the cortex results in impulsivity, social inappropriateness, and emotional dyscontrol. Often, these symptoms benefit from pharmacological and psychotherapeutic intervention. Third, patients may have emotional or functional psychological reactions to their illnesses or injuries. Common difficulties include depressive responses to the loss of cognitive capacity or vocational potential and posttraumatic stress relevant to the incident that caused the neurological insult (disease or trauma to the nervous system). Psychological problems such as these may further decrease cognitive efficiency and lead to additional neuropsychological deficits.

Although psychopharmacological treatment will not ameliorate the underlying neurological illness or structural brain damage, it may improve functional capacity or overall quality of life in neurologically involved patients. Medication can be extremely helpful in treating affective or anxiety-related symptoms of premorbid psychological disorders. In addition, psychopharmacological treatment can alleviate mood disturbance related to neurological illnesses or focal brain damage. For example, depression that follows strokes affecting the anterior portion of the dominant hemisphere, like more functional depressions, can be improved with antidepressant medication. Similarly, psychiatric medicines can be used to treat focal behavioral problems. Certain dopaminergic agonists, for instance, decrease attentional difficulties, increase productive behavior, and even increase language output.

A psychiatrist also can help avoid misdiagnosis. The consequence of misdiagnosing depression as dementia is grave, and so differentiating these two disorders is critical. Misdiagnosis can deprive the patient of appropriate treatment and lead to erroneous expectations from family and caregivers. Differentiation of traditional dementing illness (e.g., Alzheimer's disease) from cognitive decline associated with affective disturbance is best done by a psychiatrist or a psychologist approaching presenting symptoms in a systemic manner. Wells (1979) structured the symptoms of dementia and "pseudodementia" across three main areas: (a) clinical history and course, (b) complaints and clinical behavior, and (c) performance on cognitive testing.

General clinicians can benefit from referring patients to neuropsychiatrists, too. Neuropsychiatrists are conversant in the domain of psychiatry and often possess significant knowledge and skill bases in neuropathology, electrophysiology, neurochemistry, and neuropharmacology. The activity of this emerging subdiscipline is supported by the American Neuropsychiatric Association.

Physical and Occupational Therapies

Physical and occupational therapies play critical roles in the rehabilitation of neurologically involved patients. Physical therapy has traditionally had a predominant role in the treatment of gross motor and large muscle impairment and reconditioning. It has been viewed as the therapy that deals with lower extremity injuries and disturbances of gait, posture, and other whole-body movements. Meanwhile, occupational therapy has focused on the rehabilitation of fine motor difficulties and problems of the upper extremities. Occupational therapy is also concerned with remediation of functional difficulties related to activities of daily living (e.g., grooming, dressing, communication) and general adaptive difficulties brought about by associated cognitive impairments.

Today, there is an increasing amount of cotherapy and collaboration between these two disciplines, as the physical therapist and occupational therapist aid one another and optimize therapy provided by other professionals. For example, the physical therapist might address mobility issues necessary for recovery of skills needed to perform job duties, which are facilitated by the occupational therapist. The occupational therapist may assist a patient in compensating for visual field or acuity deficits, allowing for greater appreciation of visually presented materials, such as picture identification and word lists, during speech therapy sessions. Furthermore, when a patient's functional or motor impairments are the most significant problems following a neurological illness or injury, physical or occupational therapy may be more critical than even cognitive intervention provided by neurology or neuropsychology.

Speech and Language Pathology

Speech and language pathologists are heavily involved in the evaluation and treatment of cognitive disorders. In addition to evaluating developmental disorders of articulation and language, speech and language therapists with specialized training and clinical experience are critical to rehabilitative efforts directed toward stroke patients and individuals who have sustained moderate to severe traumatic brain injuries. The aphasia (gross disturbance of spoken language) that often follows such conditions requires consultation with speech therapy professionals and should be assessed prior to referring the aphasic patient to another profession.

Speech therapists address nonlanguage cognitive deficits that affect rehabilitation efforts by intervening with difficulties in verbal memory, attention, and verbal problem solving. The speech therapist should provide a comprehensive description of a patient's strengths and weaknesses in the domain of language; address the expected efficacy, anticipated type, and duration of speech therapy; and recommend home therapy to be provided by family members. A speech therapy evaluation also should establish the goals of speech and language recovery and provide prognostic information concerning language recovery.

In general, a speech and language examination and subsequent report should include the following elements:

- Evaluation of the oral musculature, including the strength and coordination of muscles of articulation.
- Thorough assessment of speech articulation characteristics and examination of speech praxis, or deficits in purposeful movement (specifically, the speech pathologist describes praxis of verbal speech and nonverbal facial movements, such as puckering lips and blowing).
- Comprehensive evaluation of all major aspects of language, including quantity of spontaneous speech, repetition, verbal comprehension, syntax, and confrontational naming, as well as written language capacity (reading and writing).
- Description of nonverbal communication capacity involving the ability to communicate by the use of facial or hand gestures and effective use of prosody (tone of voice, phrasing, voice inflection).
- Overall assessment of cognitive abilities that may be compromised by deficient language function (e.g., verbal memory, verbal reasoning).

Recreational Therapy

Recreational therapy involves treatment and recreation activities geared to individuals with illness and disability. Recreational therapists use a variety of strategies to treat or preserve the cognitive, emotional, and physical well-being of individuals with medical conditions or disability. They use games, artistic or musical activities, dance or other forms of active expression, and basic leisure time pursuits as methods to improve the motor, cognitive, and psychosocial skills of neurologically impaired individuals. In many cases, the goals are to increase a client's overall level of independence and to assist the client as he or she reintegrates into the community. Like other health care professionals, recreational therapists often work in multidisciplinary settings that include physicians, nurses, social workers, speech and language therapists, occupational therapists, physical therapists, and psychologists. Recreational therapists work especially closely with occupational therapists because of the similarity of their clinical focus.

A bachelor's degree in therapeutic recreation is typically seen as an entry-level credential for practice; some institutions offer master's or doctoral degrees as well. Coursework involves assessment, intervention, program planning, and professional ethics and often includes classroom study in abnormal psychology, anatomy, physiology, and characteristics of illness and disability. Professionals can be formally certified for practice through the National Council for Therapeutic Recreation Certification. The certification process involves obtaining a bachelor's degree in therapeutic recreation, passing a written examination, and completing an approximately 360-hr internship.

Recreational therapy services are found in general hospitals as well as inpatient and outpatient rehabilitation facilities.

Clinical Social Work

Consultation with a clinical social worker can help substantially in cases that involve psychoeducation and counseling with the client's family, interaction with community and social resources, and placement issues. Social workers have a strong understanding of and familiarity with resources and are well trained to communicate the resource needs of a client to the family and other caregivers. They are able to enlist families as patient advocates in procuring financial support, follow-up services, and equipment for long-term care. Social workers are instrumental in coordinating and integrating various aspects of evaluation and treatment services. Indeed, social workers are often most valuable in ensuring continuity of care for patients who require the services of diverse professionals—psychologists, physical therapists, legal counsel, and so on. In turn, social workers synthesize assorted information and evaluation findings from various professionals to provide greater awareness and relevance for family and caregivers. Finally, a clinical social worker can convey a patient's strengths, weaknesses, and supervision needs, thereby answering family members' questions about what level of supervision a patient requires and about their own abilities and resources to care for their family member.

Hospital-based social workers often have extensive experience with specific medical and neurological populations, such as stroke or TBI patients. Contacting a rehabilitation facility is the most effective way to enlist a social worker with the requisite background for a client's specific needs.

Vocational Rehabilitation

Vocational rehabilitation counselors provide services to individuals with physical or cognitive disabilities that present challenges in returning to the workplace. A vocational rehabilitation counselor's initial assessment focuses on the client's educational and vocational history and experience as well as the nature and magnitude of the client's present cognitive and physical capacities. Along with an interview, the assessment may include formal testing related to vocational skills and interests. This information is integrated into an individual rehabilitation plan that specifies which services are required for the patient to meet his or her rehabilitation goals. The individual rehabilitation plan is often detailed and specifies such services as additional, focused assessment of vocational aptitudes; referral to other professions (e.g., neurology, psychology) for ancillary examination or assessment services; continuing education or specialized training; assistance in obtaining necessary adaptive devices or assistive technologies; work adjustment training; and job placement and follow-up. Vocational rehabilitation services can help the general clinician and his or her client clarify psychotherapeutic goals; plan for the stresses that accompany vocational reentry; and increase self-efficacy, self-esteem, and quality of life.

Training for vocational rehabilitation occurs through both undergraduate and graduate programs and often includes curricula related to the theory and practice of vocational rehabilitation; physical, cognitive, emotional, and other aspects of disability; vocational evaluation strategies; approaches to job analysis and placement resources; topics related to special populations; case management strategies; and practical field placement experiences.

Vocational rehabilitation counselors work in a variety of private and public settings, including state vocational rehabilitation agencies, independent living centers, and veterans' programs, as well as rehabilitation hospitals and technical colleges.

Conclusion

General clinicians should have a conversational understanding of the role of all professionals who work with individuals who have neurological impairment. Such an understanding assists in making appropriate referrals for initial evaluation and in utilizing intervention services managed by the psychologist following the neuropsychological evaluation. Awareness of other professional roles facilitates communication between professionals; increases the confidence the specialists have in psychological services; and leads to more integrated, seamless service delivery on the part of the clinician. An appreciation of related fields is even more necessary given the emerging role of psychologists in primary-care settings.

Additional Reading

Textbooks such as *Fundamentals of Human Neuropsychology* (4th ed., Kolb & Whishaw, 1996), *Neuropsychology: A Clinical Approach* (3rd ed., Walsh, 1994), and *Clinical Neuropsychology* (3rd ed., Heilman & Valenstein, 1993) provide fuller coverage of general topics in neuropsychology. A comprehensive source for information in the subspecialty of geriatric clinical neuropsychology is *Geriatric Neuropsychology* by Albert and Moss (1988).

2

Basic Functional
Neuroanatomy

Although this book is not intended to provide comprehensive coverage of clinical neuroscience or neuroanatomy,
a review of basic functional neuroanatomic divisions is necessary. General clinicians must have some understanding of
the various neurobehavioral syndromes they encounter. Such
understanding enriches clinical awareness, improves communication with specialists, and fosters improved treatment
of neurologically involved clients.

Overview of the Central Nervous System

The central nervous system (CNS) comprises the brain and
the spinal cord. The brain can be conceptualized as three
structures that represent hierarchical activity of the CNS: (a)
the brain stem, (b) the subcortex, and (c) the cerebral cortex.
The spinal cord is a mediator between spinal nerves and the
brain. It possesses nerve fibers that relay sensory (e.g., vision,
hearing) information to the brain and motor (movement) information from the brain to the rest of the body. Several other
supportive elements and systems play important roles in the
CNS.

Structure of the Neuron

The building block of the CNS is the neuron, or nerve cell. Each neuron (like other types of cells) contains a number of structures, known as *organelles,* that perform various maintenance and action functions. The neuron is surrounded by the cell membrane, which is semipermeable and allows monitored transport of various substances in and out of the cell. The cell membrane is composed of double lipid (fatlike) layers, embedded with special proteins that regulate which chemical substances cross the membrane. Within the boundaries supplied by the cell membrane is a jellylike semiliquid termed *cytoplasm.* Other important structures within the neuron are the *soma, dendrites,* the *axon,* and *synapses.* Figure 2.1 is a diagram of the basic structures of the neuron.

Soma

The soma, or cell body, contains most of the cell's organelles, which determine its structure and function (see Figure 2.2).

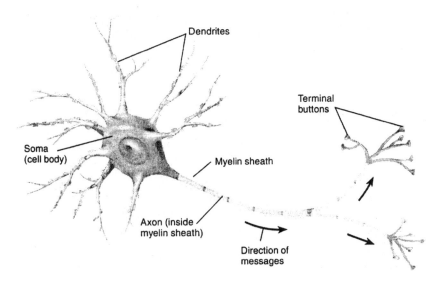

Figure 2.1. Major structures of the multipolar neuron.

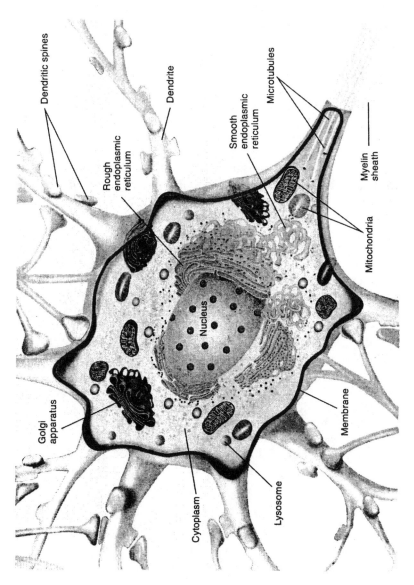

Figure 2.2.   Primary organelles of the cell.

A major function of the soma is the manufacture and transportation of substances, such as proteins, that are required to maintain the cell or that act as neurotransmitters (Martin, 1998). Important organelles within the soma are explained below.

- *Nucleus*—a structure that is critical to cell functions such as reproduction and protein synthesis. The nucleus contains the nucleolus and chromosomes. The nucleolus manufactures ribosomal ribonucleic acid (RNA), which participates in the formation of proteins. Chromosomes are composed of deoxyribonucleic acid (DNA), which is the genetic material of the cell. DNA controls the growth and development of the cell into its mature form.
- *Endoplasmic reticulum*—a storage and transmission reservoir that appears in two types: rough and smooth. Rough endoplasmic reticulum is so termed because of the irregular appearance when ribosomes become attached to the surface. Protein produced by the ribosomes is destined for transport out of the cell. Smooth endoplasmic reticulum is concerned with transport within the cell.
- *Ribosomes*—RNA- and protein-rich structures within the cell that are the site of protein synthesis.
- *Golgi apparatus*—a type of smooth endoplasmic reticulum that functions to collect proteins from the rough endoplasmic reticulum and cover them with a membrane, thus packaging them for transport out of the cell.
- *Lysosomes*—contain enzymes that degrade a wide variety of substances that originate both inside and outside the cell. They may leave a residue called *lipofuscin granules*, which appear in cells in increasing concentration with aging.
- *Mitochondria*—produce energy required by most of the functions of the cell. They have a characteristic cigar shape, with a smooth outer surface and a folded internal structure. Brain cells derive all of their energy from glucose, which is extracted from the blood as needed. However, the brain has no mechanism for glucose storage, thus the deprivation of glucose results in rapid cell death. The mitochondria take up glucose and break it

down to form adenosine triphosphate. Another function of the mitochondria is the storage of calcium, which is used in regulating the release of transmitter substances from the terminals of one neuron to other neurons.

☐ *Microtubules*—fiberlike structures within the cell that are responsible for transportation of proteins to different parts of the cell. This transportation can take many forms, including orthograde transport (from the soma to distal parts of the neuron), retrograde transport (from distal regions to the soma), and fast or slow axoplasmic transport (fast can move only in one direction, slow can move toward or away from the soma).

☐ *Microfilaments*—threadlike structures involved in controlling the shape, movement, or fluidity of the cytoplasm.

Dendrites

Dendrites are treelike structures that receive neural messages from sending cells. In some cases, the soma may actually receive the message. The general function of the dendrite is to exponentially increase the surface area of the cell. Dendrites posses dendritic spines, which are rough appendages sprouting from the individual dendrites.

A striking feature of the dendrite is the ability to grow and change throughout the life span. The alteration of dendritic processes may represent some aspects of the cellular substrate of learning. Conversely, mental retardation and dementias are associated with reduced dendritic length or a reduced number of dendritic spines.

Axon

The axon is a long, slender tube often covered with myelin sheath, which can be thought of as a source of insulation to the neuron, similar to the rubber coating of an electrical wire. The axon originates in the cell body at a point called the *axon hillock* and is responsible for carrying information away from the cell body to a point at which the neural message is transmitted to the dendrites and spines of other neurons.

Most axons have branches at the end called *collaterals*. At the end of the collaterals are fine terminations called *telodendria*. The telodendria, in turn, lead to tiny knobs called *terminals*, which form junctions with other cells. Like dendrites, the axon can grow other telodendria and terminals, and this growth process also may play a role in learning. Although the cell has only one axon, the axon can grow many telodendria, which allow a single message to be sent to many destinations.

Synapses

A synapse is the connection between two neurons at which a nervous impulse passes from one neuron to the other. A small space between neurons, known as the *synaptic cleft*, typically exists, but it is possible for two neurons to actually touch. Figure 2.3 shows the synaptic junction.

The Brain

The brain is the most important part of the nervous system. It consists of the brain stem, the subcortex, and the cerebral cortex. In this section I discuss these individually, along with their components, and then provide a brief explanation of brain development and a theory of brain function.

Brain Stem

The brain stem is located at the top of the spinal cord. As it enters the skull, the spinal cord enlarges and differentiates anatomically to form the three major components of the brain stem: (a) the medulla, (b) the pons, and (c) the midbrain. The basic structures of the brain stem are illustrated in Figure 2.4. The brain stem resembles the spinal cord in function and appearance but is considerably more elaborate and complex.

An integral structure that runs through the entire brain stem is the *reticular formation*. Neurons within the reticular formation create a netlike configuration that mediates com-

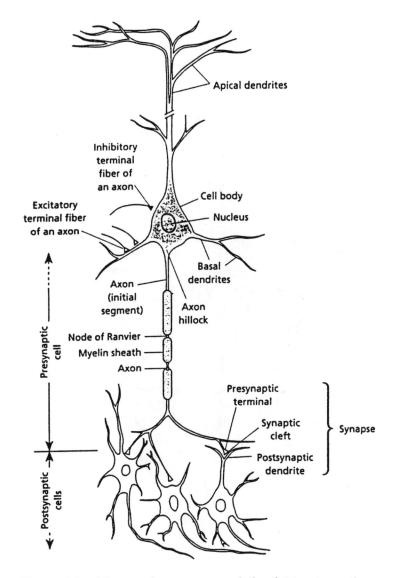

Figure 2.3.   Neuronal processes and dendritic connections.

munication among the spinal cord, cerebellum, cerebral cortex, and other brain structures. A specific feature of the reticular formation is the division of the reticular activating system. The ascending reticular activating system receives in-

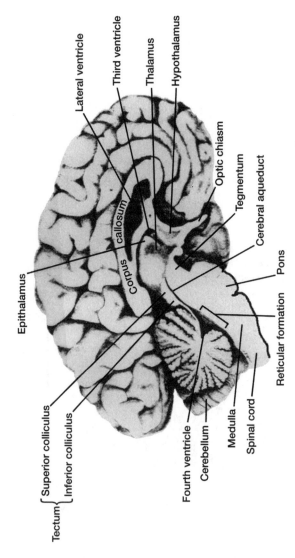

Figure 2.4.   Brainstem structures as revealed by a medial view of the brain.

formation from the various sensory systems (e.g., touch, vision) and interfaces with the spinal cord. The descending reticular activating system is a second pathway that originates in the frontal part of the cortex and sends messages down to the brain stem. Together, these two mechanisms allow us to be alerted by meaningful sights, sounds, or touches in our environment. It is the ascending system that allows one to hear an intruder open a window when one is in the midst of a deep sleep. Alternately, it is the descending system that permits the planning and reasoning part of the cortex to increase one's attention and alertness during an important exam in school. Collectively, the ascending and descending reticular activating systems form a general monitoring apparatus that is crucial in the maintenance of wakefulness, consciousness, and attention.

Although the entire brain stem contributes to the functioning of the reticular activating system, the brain stem's three components are independently responsible for other functions. The *midbrain* performs several unique and specialized functions. Visual information, for example, is initially relayed to the midbrain. While visual details of what we view are ultimately processed in the rear portion of the cerebral cortex, various visual reflexes originate in the midbrain. Blinking, dilation and constriction of the pupil, and certain eye movements are organized in the midbrain. Certain hearing reflexes, such as being startled by a loud or unfamiliar noise, also originate in this region. The midbrain also organizes basic movement patterns, such as walking and running. The midbrain does not contain systems that enable an individual to make a voluntary or deliberate decision to move or refrain from moving.

Just below the midbrain is the *pons*, a large bulge in the brain stem. The center of the pons contains a substantial portion of the reticular system, including some neurons necessary for the regulation of the sleep–wake cycle. The upper portion of the pons plays a role in wakefulness, and a mechanism in the lower part of the pons permits one to fall asleep. The pons is responsible for the vital inhibition of motor activity that accompanies certain stages of sleep. Without this control, one would become highly active during sleep and possibly hurt oneself.

The anatomically lowest structure of the brain stem is the *medulla*, or *medulla oblongata*. The medulla contains a segment of the reticular formation, and it controls such primitive yet life-sustaining functions as regulation of the cardiovascular system, breathing, and maintenance of muscular tone in the skeletal muscles. The medulla also contributes to more subtle processes. The medulla has been implicated as a mechanism that assists in reducing the body's sensitivity to pain. It was shown in the late 1960s that surgical implantation of a probe that provides electrical stimulation of the medulla could produce analgesia (decreased pain sensitivity). This procedure is available to reduce chronic, unavoidable pain that might otherwise incapacitate a person. A final function of the medulla involves its contribution to some types of classical conditioning. For example, research in the early 1980s showed that damage to a region of the medulla, termed the *inferior olive*, prevented acquisition of a conditioned eyeblink. This suggests that one's ability to associate some cue with a forthcoming puff of air directed to the eye is abolished by damage to a specific region of the medulla. It is interesting that this implies that even this relatively primitive brain structure has some part in learning new responses.

Subcortex

Although debate exists regarding the structures that compose the subcortical region, the cerebellum, hypothalamus, thalamus basal ganglia, and limbic system are often viewed as resident to the subcortex.

Cerebellum. The *cerebellum*, which is not technically a subcortical structure, is positioned behind the medulla and below the posterior portion of the cerebral cortex. Historically, the cerebellum was seen almost exclusively as responsible for fine motor control and coordination. It is now recognized that cerebellar damage manifests as relatively diverse motor symptoms. The symptoms that are exhibited depend on the region of the cerebellum that was disturbed. For example, damage to the vermis region (a structure in the middle of the cerebellum) may produce postural disturbance, whereas lateral lesions may result in difficulty coordinating rapid alternating (ballistic) movements. Damage to other cerebellar regions can cause vertigo and disturbance of eye movements. The cerebellum participates in higher cognitive skills as well. Specifically, it contributes to aspects of perceptual responses (Leiner, Leiner, & Dow, 1989), planning and judgment of time, and learning and memory (Mayes, 1988).

Hypothalamus. The *hypothalamus* serves basic regulatory functions related to thirst, appetite, and sexual arousal (Saper, 1990). Lesions to various regions of the hypothalamus produce a variety of symptoms, including diminished drive states, obesity, and loss of or decreased temperature regulation. Mood states also are impacted by hypothalamic lesions (Shepherd, 1988).

Thalamus. An oval-shaped structure, the *thalamus* lies near the middle of the brain and is composed of two distinct halves. Each half includes at least 11 major nuclei (groups of cell bodies) that relay information between higher and lower motor and sensory regions. The thalamus has been described as a way station for most sensory pathways to the cerebral cortex, and it contributes significantly to the conscious experience of sensation (Brodal, 1981). The thalamus also plays a critical role in higher cortical functions, such as language and memory (Crosson, 1992). In the area of memory, both new learning and the recall of previously acquired information may be compromised following thalamic lesions (Butters & Albert, 1982). Although little evidence exists to suggest that thalamic damage produces a true aphasia, Crosson (1992) asserted that typical symptoms include decreased verbal fluency, spontaneity of speech, and reduced tone. Right thalamic lesions often result in decreased visual perceptual abilities, and thalamic damage may contribute to emotional alterations such as reduced spontaneity, apathy, or lowered initiative (Butters & Stuss, 1989).

Basal ganglia. At the base of the cerebral hemispheres is a collection of nuclear masses termed the *basal ganglia*. Three critical structures within the basal ganglia are the *putamen*, the *caudate*, and the *globus pallidus*. The basal ganglia serve as a principal motoric control center and participate in voluntary and automatic movements. The structures of the basal ganglia can be regarded as one component of the larger system that translates cognition into action (Passingham, 1987). The basal ganglia also contribute to learning and memory and receptive and expressive language (Crosson, 1992).

Limbic system. The limbic system (see Figure 2.5) consists of several structures that add to the regulation of emotion (Mesulam, 2000). Limbic structures in addition to the hypothalamus include the cingulate, septal region, hippocampus, fornix, and amygdala. These structures regulate and adjust the emotional tone that accompanies behavior and contributes to motivational aspects of behavior and learning and memory. Indeed, lesion to the *cingulate* often brings about an amotivational or akinetic syndrome in which patients display almost no initiation of behavior and will at times simply sit for hours. The *septal region* has a significant role in the expression of intense anger or rage. Playing a critical role in learning and memory, the *hippocampus* consolidates new information and contributes to the transition of short-term to long-term memory formation. The *fornix*, an exceptionally large fiber bundle that originates in the hippocampus, is a critical interconnection for neurocircuitry within the limbic system. Finally, the *amygdala* plays a mediating role in the expression of emotional responses and participates in the laying down of new learning, especially of information or events that have a strong emotional component.

Cerebral Cortex

The cerebral cortex is the newest and most developed portion of the brain. It participates in the highest level of cognitive processing and contributes substantially to aspects of personality and social interaction. Although many methods for distinguishing the functional areas of the cortex have been proposed, the most basic divisions of the cortex are into its two hemispheres or its four lobes—occipital, parietal, temporal, and frontal. The breakdown of the cortex into four lobes has flourished primarily because of the convenience it affords clinicians and researchers (see Figure 2.5). (Brodmann [1909] offered another way to classify the functions of the cortex that is often cited and is based on differences among its cells.)

Left and right hemispheres. Although primary sensory and motor centers hold corresponding positions within the two cortical hemispheres (Lezak, 1995), control of other functions overlaps between the hemispheres or is more principally provided by one hemisphere or the other.

The left hemisphere, in most right-handed individuals, is dominant for learning purposeful or skilled motor movement sequences and for comprehending and expressing language. In left-handed individuals, left-hemisphere dominance for language is less pronounced: Only about 70 percent of left-handed persons are definitively left-hemisphere dominant for language. Organizing information within temporal or sequential contexts also is a predominantly left-hemisphere mediated function (Luria, 1980; Mateer, 1983).

The right hemisphere is associated with nonverbal aspects of processing the environment. It is most involved in visuospatial perceptual functioning, including analyzing relative depth, discerning figure–ground relations, recognizing human faces, and integrating body image within the larger environment. In addition, the right hemisphere helps allocate attentional resources to specific sensory targets. Right-hemisphere dysfunction often leads to hemi-attentional deficits of the left visual field. Whereas the left hemisphere contributes dominantly to verbal aspects of language, the right hemisphere is superior in processing paraverbal or nonverbal elements of communication. The right hemisphere supports one's understanding of facial expressions, emotional tone, postural or gestural cues, and prosody of speech. It also aids in one's appreciation of music and melodic line. Indeed, damage to the right hemisphere often brings about *amusia*, or perceptual loss for musical stimuli.

Occipital lobe. The most significant responsibilities of the *occipital lobe* are analysis and integration of visual stimuli. Following initial reception within the retina, visual information is relayed to the thalamus and then to the occipital lobe,

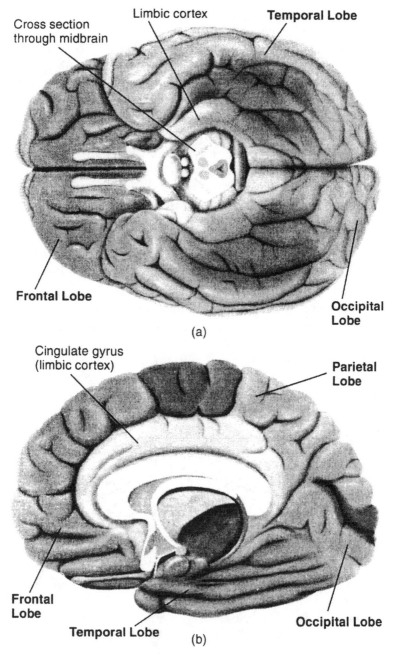

Figure 2.5.   The four cortical lobes of the brain.

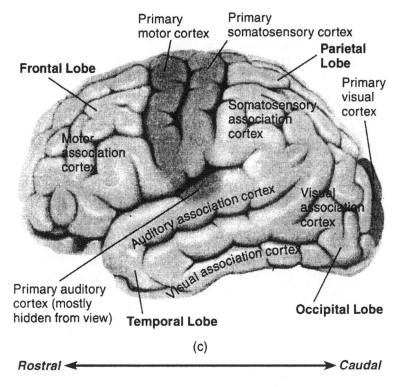

Figure 2.5. *Continued*

where it is processed at increasingly complex levels. Simple cells in the occipital lobe fire to only one elementary characteristic (e.g., vertical lines) of a stimulus. Complex cells respond to angled lines. Hypercomplex cells respond to combinations of basic stimuli that form complex visual configurations (Hubel & Wiesel, 1968). Visual information is processed in the striate cortex of the occipital lobe and then relayed to association areas where more synthetic processing occurs. Following analysis within the occipital lobe, information is passed to the parietal lobe, which plays a role in visuospatial location or object positioning, or the temporal lobe, which provides object recognition and analysis of form and shape. In addition to its role with visual stimuli, the occipital lobe contains the neuronal capacity to process tactile, auditory, and vestibular input (Jung, 1961).

Parietal lobe. The *parietal lobe* processes tactile stimuli, kinesthetic stimuli, and proprioceptive stimuli (information used to coordinate muscular activity). Parietal cortex is composed of diverse cell types that are responsive to a variety of stimuli, including one's own movement, hand position when reaching for something, audition, eye movement, and complex visual stimuli (Joseph, 1990). Processing somesthetic information (bodily sensations) is a critical function of the parietal lobe. The segment of the parietal lobe dedicated to this task is known as the *primary sensory cortex*, or the *sensory strip*. The body is topographically represented by the cells of the sensory strip. The lower body (trunk, leg, foot, etc.) is represented along the medial portion of the strip, whereas the upper body and face are represented along the lateral portions of the strip. In this way, the entire body is represented on the brain's surface. Body regions that demand greater sensory importance are given greater cortical representation. For example, because of the high sensory and motor demands inherent in speech movements, the lips and tongue are given greater cortical representation than a larger body part such as the back.

Parietal lesion can result in significant somatosensory deficits and other clinical syndromes, including deficits in body sense, visuospatial orientation, and temporal–sequential motor activity; anomia (inability to name common objects); disruption of writing; and acalculia (mathematical impairment). In addition, lesions to one hemisphere of the parietal lobe produce attention problems related to stimuli presented in the opposite half of visual space. This is particularly prevalent with lesions to the right hemisphere. The inferior, or lower, portion of the parietal lobe of the dominant hemisphere contributes significantly to symbolic or linguistic processing, such as interpreting alphanumeric information. As such, a lesion to this portion of the parietal lobe can lead to deficits in reading, writing, and certain aspects of mathematical abilities.

Temporal lobe. The *temporal lobe* has a variety of cognitive functions but is principally involved in processing auditory information. Following initial sensory integration in the primary auditory area (Heschyl's gyrus), auditory information is integrated at increasingly complex levels to produce the perceptual phenomenon necessary to appreciate complex aural stimuli, such as musical melody or human speech. The right temporal region is generally superior to the left in integrating nonverbal stimuli, such as music; recognizing paraverbal aspects of communication, such as tone or rhythm of human speech; and appreciating environmental stimuli, such as a barking dog or running engine. Alternately, the left temporal region has greater priority in processing speech sounds. Fundamental aspects of the speech signal are analyzed in the primary auditory cortex within the temporal lobe and then synthesized in posterior areas of the temporal lobe into hierarchically more complex elements of speech (i.e., words, phrases). One such posterior area, known as *Wernicke's area*, is critical for comprehension—extracting meaning from human speech.

A second major role of the temporal lobe relates to memory. Buried in medial regions of the temporal lobe is the hippocampus. As explained earlier, the hippocampus, with surrounding tissue, transfers recent (short-term) memories into long-term storage in modality-specific areas of the cortex. In other words, the memory of the pattern of a rug is likely to be stored in the visual cortex. As with other aspects of sensory and cognitive function, memory functions are lateralized in the two hemispheres. The left temporal region predominates in the storage of verbal material, and the right temporal region lays away nonverbal, visual–spatial memories.

Frontal lobe. The frontal lobe has been viewed historically as the "seat of intelligence"—responsible for the highest of cognitive faculties, but this view is somewhat extravagant. Work as early as Zangwill's (1966) and K. Goldstein's (1944) suggests that intelligence is minimally affected by even relatively large lesions to the frontal lobes. Depending on the specific areas of the frontal lobe that are affected, damage to the frontal region can bring about very different cognitive or behavioral consequences. In this regard, the simplistic notion of a single frontal syndrome has been abandoned in favor of the broader conceptualization of a family of frontal syndromes. This view is supported by recognition of and attention to four major functional–anatomical areas of the frontal lobe: the *primary motor cortex* (Brodmann's areas 4, 6, 8, 44, and 45), the *dorsolateral prefrontal cortex* (9, 10, 11, 45, 46, and 47), the *lateral orbital cortex* (10, 11, 12, 13, and 14), and the *anterior cingulate cortex*. Damage to any of these areas results in a distinct constellation of cognitive and behavioral patterns. Damage to the primary motor cortex leads mostly to motor deficits, whereas damage to the dorsolateral prefrontal, orbital, and anterior (medial) cingulate areas produces affective, behavioral, and cognitive effects. The regions are depicted in Figure 2.6.

Cummings (1993) identified three subcortical–frontal circuits that, when damaged, result in distinctive neurobehavioral sequelae (see Figure 2.7). These circuits involve frontal areas, basal ganglia structures, and regions of the thalamus. Table 2.1 illustrates the unique cognitive and emotional changes that occur as a result of damage to these systems.

Brain Development

The process of brain growth and differentiation consists of a series of changes that occur in a relatively fixed sequence.

□ *Cell formation and migration*—In the fetus, nerve cells form by division in the interior, or ventricular, lining of the brain and then migrate outward. Division concludes during the middle of gestation. Migration may extend postnatally.

□ *Formation and growth of axons*—Axons begin sprouting from neurons as the neurons migrate to their targets. Sprouting axons grow in a given direction due to the orientation of the cell or other, unknown, factors. The growing end is called the *growth cone*.

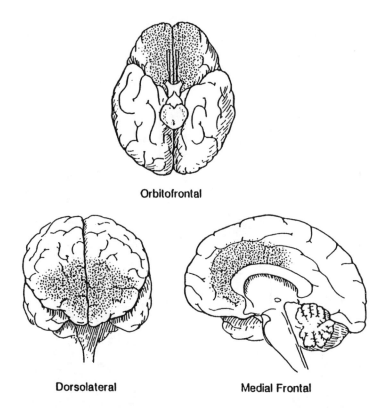

Figure 2.6. Frontal regions affected in orbitofrontal, dorsolateral, and medial frontal syndromes.

□ *Formation of dendrites*—After a neuron reaches its final position in the cortex, dendrites are formed and grow at a relatively slow rate. A proliferation of dendritic development—indeed, overdevelopment—leads to pruning of dendrites and shedding of dendritic spines.

□ *Formation of synaptic connections*—In humans, synaptic density increases until age 2 and then decreases 50% by age 16. Synapses survive if their activity correlates with that of neighboring cells.

□ *Myelination*—Insulating cells around neurons develop hierarchically, with regions of the frontal lobes being the last to become myelinated. Myelination, in some cases, is not complete until after the onset of adolescence.

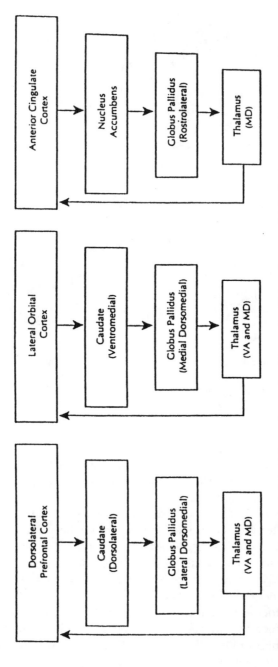

Figure 2.7.   Organization of the three frontal–subcortical circuits in which lesions produce cognitive and behavioral change. VA = Ventral Anterior; MD = Medial Dorsal.

Table 2.1

Clinical Features of Frontal Lobe Syndromes

Location	Features
Orbitofrontal	Disinhibition
	Inappropriate affect
	Impaired judgment and insight
	Distractibility
Dorsolateral	Executive function deficits
	Perseveration
	Stimulus-bound behavior
	Diminished verbal fluency
Medial frontal	Apathy
	Mutism or transcortical motor aphasia
	Lower extremity paresis
	Incontinence

Note. From "Frontal Subcortical Circuits and Human Behavior" by J. L. Cummings, 1993, *Archives of Neurology, 50*, pp. 873–880. Copyright 1993 by the American Medical Association. Adapted with permission.

Lurian Theory of Brain Function

Three predominating theories of brain function that have developed through the years are localizationist, equipotentialist, and modular or hierarchical (Lurian). *Localizationist* theory maintains that specific regions of the cortex have a point-to-point relationship with equally focal behaviors or capacities. In *equipotentialist* theory, all brain tissue makes similar contributions to various functions or capacities, meaning that a specific behavioral deficit is related more to the volume of tissue damage than to the specific location of the lesion. Hughlings Jackson cast doubt on strict localization of complex cognitive activity, a perspective that was taken up more extensively by Aleksandr Luria.

The current view of cognitive functioning was predicated

by Luria's theory. Luria argued that brain–behavior relations are modular and interactional. In Luria's framework, the brain consists of three primary units. The first unit is responsible for basic arousal, activation, and cortical tone. A second unit receives sensory–perceptual input (via auditory, visual, tactile, and other modalities) and subsequently processes such input at increasingly complex levels prior to long-term storage. The third unit prepares plans, motor responses, and other behavioral actions appropriate for dealing with the environment at large.

Luria also asserted that the brain is organized in a hierarchical fashion, with information being processed at primary, secondary, and tertiary zones. Each of the three functional units contains these three hierarchically arranged zones, with every zone contributing in different ways to aspects of arousal: receiving, perceptually processing and storing information, and organizing responses for motor or behavioral output into the environment.

The primary zones are responsible for the most basic level of analysis. Using vision as an example, the primary visual zone processes elemental visual stimuli, such as the angle of a given light or bands of higher or lower illumination that provide basic information on elements of shadow. The primary visual cortex is found at the back of the brain, in the occipital lobe. Following analysis of basic aspects of visual input from the retina within the primary visual cortex, complex visual analysis takes place in the secondary visual zone. Here, the basic elements of angles or areas of light and dark are synthesized and perceptually organized in a more complex way. At the tertiary level, visual information is processed with nonvisual perceptual input (e.g., the feel of a cube in one's hand). Tertiary cortex is cross-modal in nature, allowing the integration of multimodal perceptual information. Tertiary regions allow one to recognize an object placed in one's hand (e.g., key, coin, paper clip) even when one is unable to see the object. The tertiary cortex is found within the inferior parietal lobe and the frontal lobe.

The hierarchical model of Luria allows a more accurate method for evaluating the impact of neurological injury or illness. The model supports a modular view of neuropsy-chological status, in which various cognitive functions are not strictly localized in a single, rigidly circumscribed region. Rather, complex cognitive abilities (e.g., reading) are sub-served by networks of separate brain regions, which may be geographically distant from one another.

Supportive Elements and Systems

Given the importance of the CNS and its relatively high met-abolic demands, a great burden is placed on supportive ele-ments and maintenance functions. Glial cells (also called *neu-roglia* and *glia*), cerebrospinal fluid, and meninges provide physical support and protection to the vulnerable and fragile brain. In addition, the neuroglia assist in regularly removing metabolic waste products and debris collected within the brain. Moreover, the brain's high oxygen and glucose require-ments necessitate an elaborate cerebrovascular system, which provides these elements via the blood supply.

Glial Cells

Glial cells, such as astrocytes, oligodendrocytes, and micro-glia, perform critical maintenance functions within the CNS. Specifically, various types of glia add physical support and cohesion to relatively fragile neuronal structures, provide in-sulation that allows for isolated communication among neu-ral substrates, and remove metabolic wastes that accrue within the CNS. Different types of glial cells have relatively specialized functions.

Astrocytes are star-shaped glial cells that maintain contact with both neurons and capillaries, suggesting that these two entities may exchange certain substances. Astrocytes provide structural support and assist in regulating and removing cer-tain chemicals discharged during previous neural commu-nication. Astrocytes also assist during brain development by forming a basic framework that axons can follow as they extend outward.

Oligodendrocytes are glial cells that comprise a central soma with many paddle-shaped processes that form one segment of myelin sheath that encases multiple CNS neurons. Myelin comprises both lipid and protein layers and insulates neuronal tissue as a means of increasing effectiveness and speed of neural transmission. (Schwann cells perform a similar function to oligodendrocytes, but in the peripheral nervous system.)

Microglia are simply a variety of oligodendrocytes, some argue. The primary function of the microglia is phagocytosis, in which these glial cells essentially consume debris (e.g., dead cells) by engulfing the substance and ultimately digesting it. When injury occurs to an area of the brain, the number and activity level of microglia increase precipitously.

Ventricular System

The ventricular system is responsible for the production and circulation of cerebrospinal fluid (CSF). Among other functions, CSF reduces the brain's overall weight and dampens shock to the nervous system as a result of sudden head movement. The ventricular system comprises a series of interconnected chambers, or ventricles, through which CSF passes. There are four ventricles: two lateral ventricles and the more centrally positioned third and fourth ventricles. After passing through the ventricles and the passages connecting these structures, CSF flows through a set of openings into the subarachnoid space, where it is reabsorbed into the blood supply. When a part of this system is obstructed and CSF cannot flow freely, the CSF becomes congested and leads to an increase in intracranial pressure, termed *hydrocephalus*, which requires immediate medical intervention. The ventricular system is depicted in Figure 2.8.

Vascular System

Because of the brain's high metabolic demand for blood and oxygen, it receives 20% of the heart's total blood supply. The brain's ability to independently store glucose or extract energy without available oxygen is limited. When the brain does not receive enough glucose and oxygen, unconsciousness results within a matter of seconds, and permanent brain damage ensues within a few minutes. The brain's blood supply arrives by means of two primary sources: the internal carotid arteries and the vertebral arteries. The internal carotid system comprises two principal vessels—the anterior cerebral artery and the middle cerebral artery—that branch to form numerous smaller vessels. The anterior cerebral artery distributes blood to the frontal region as well as some aspects of the medial surface of the brain, and the middle cerebral artery supplies the largest segment of the lateral surface of each hemisphere of the brain. The vertebral arteries first join to form the basilar artery, then branch off to form smaller arteries that irrigate the cerebellum before giving rise to the posterior cerebral artery. The posterior cerebral artery distribution is focused principally on the occipital and inferior temporal lobe tissue. The cortical regions supplied by each of the three principal cerebral arteries can be seen in Figure 2.9.

Meninges

Although the skull provides much protection to the underlying brain, the delicate composition of neural tissue and the irregular and rough interior surfaces of some regions of the cranium necessitate additional supportive layers, called *meninges*. Both the brain and spinal cord are covered by these tough connective layers. The three types of meninges are the dura mater, the arachnoid layer, and the pia mater. The *dura mater*, the outermost layer, is a relatively stiff covering that assists in cushioning the underlying brain. The *arachnoid layer* is a weblike structure through which cerebral arteries traverse. The *pia mater*, the innermost layer, closely conforms to the contours of the brain, providing support for the gelatinous brain matter. The meningeal layers are depicted in Figure 2.10.

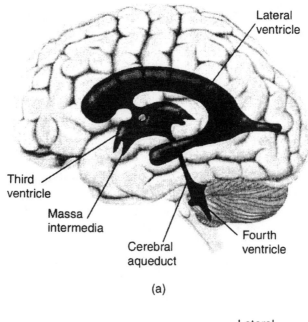

(a)

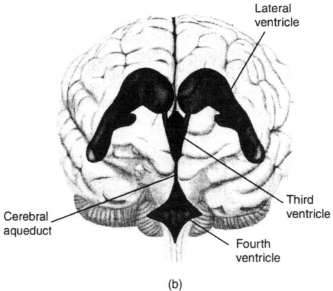

(b)

Figure 2.8.   The ventricular system.

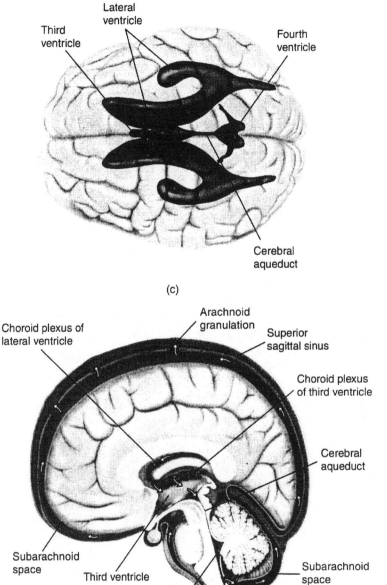

(c)

(d)

Figure 2.8. *Continued*

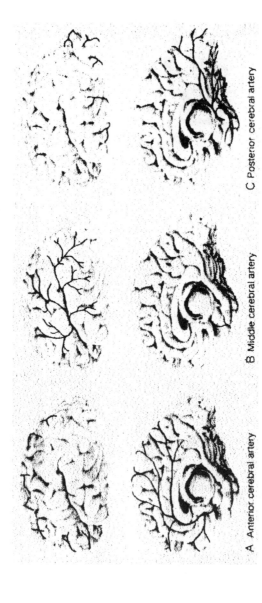

A Anterior cerebral artery   B Middle cerebral artery   C Posterior cerebral artery

Figure 2.9.   Lateral (top) and medial (bottom) views of the distribution of major cerebral arteries in the cortical hemispheres.

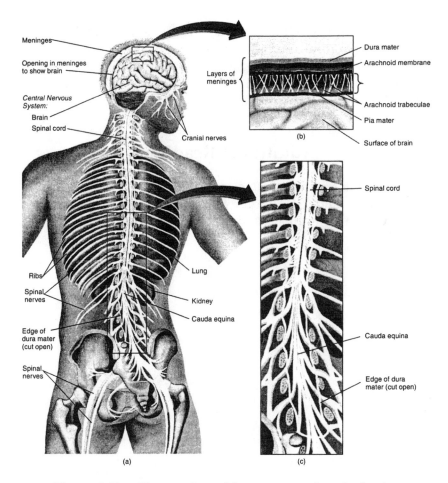

Figure 2.10.   The meningeal layers protecting the brain.

Conclusion

Although an exhaustive understanding of all aspects of neuroanatomy and neurophysiology is not required, a general conceptualization of brain structure and function is important for general clinicians in making appropriate referrals for neuropsychological evaluation and services. Such an understanding allows more accurate screening and subsequent referral of individuals with potential neurological or developmental conditions. In addition, a rudimentary understanding of neurobehavioral mechanisms serves the clinician well as he or she attempts to navigate the often-bewildering landscape of the medical record and case history of clients with known brain injury or disease.

Additional Reading

Neuroanatomy and Neuropathology: A Clinical Guide for Neuropsychologists (2nd ed., Reitan & Wolfson, 1992) is an illustrated volume that deals with basic neuroanatomy.

II

Neurological Conditions

3

Neurobehavioral Syndromes in General Practice

Neurological conditions can produce significant cognitive or psychological changes. An understanding of common neurological conditions that can affect behavior or clinical presentation assists general clinicians in detecting problems that may have a neurological basis and referring clients for appropriate services.

Head Trauma

Head trauma, or traumatic brain injury (TBI), can be a debilitating condition with enormous impact on the patient, family, and society at large. The incidence rate in the United States is estimated at 400,000 new cases annually. Because of advancements in surgical and medical interventions, many patients now survive injuries that previously would have resulted in death. The epidemiological literature consistently reveals that head trauma is a tremendous public health problem that results in numerous behavioral and neuropsychological symptoms for patients, devastating fallout for families of patients, and extensive economic repercussions for society in general.

Head trauma can be categorized as closed or open. A closed head injury is less likely than an open injury to involve subsequent infectious processes, but other neuropathologic processes are more likely with closed head injury. There is a greater tendency for increased intracranial pressure, development of hematomas and edema, and posttraumatic hydrocephalus. Delayed-onset effects of the TBI include formation of a subdural hematoma, seizure disorder and, less commonly, progressive dementia. It has been hypothesized that head trauma increases the chances that an individual will develop Alzheimer's disease later in life (Plassman et al., 2000). Other forms of dementia related to head trauma are sometimes observed in younger individuals.

In general, TBI produces diffuse neuropathologic changes; however, some specific neuroanatomic regions are particularly vulnerable to the effects of acceleration–deceleration injuries, such as those that occur in motor vehicle collisions. Two cortical regions that are susceptible to focal damage are the orbital frontal region (area of frontal lobe above the eyes) and the anterior portion of the temporal lobe. These areas are more prone to damage because of their direct contact with a particularly irregular and rough interior surface of the cranium. As the frontal and temporal lobes are forced against the interior of the front of the skull, significant amounts of shearing and contusion occur in these regions. The area of direct impact is commonly referred to as the *coup*. When the brain is also forced against the inner surface of the skull at a point opposite to the primary coup, that is a *contra-coup* injury (Alexander, 1987).

An additional source of damage in TBI is diffuse axonal injury, which results from the rapid acceleration–deceleration or rotational movements of the brain within the cranial vault. Lesions produced in this manner most dramatically affect the long white-matter tracts. Damage to the corpus callosum and rostral brain stem are common.

The immediate effect of the injuries noted above is loss of consciousness or a period of coma ranging from a few minutes to many days. Following the coma, the patient regains awareness of his or her surroundings to varying degrees. Although the patient may exhibit general awareness, a period of posttraumatic amnesia (PTA) often occurs. During PTA, the patient has no consistent recall for events that have occurred during the previous hours or days. Length of coma and PTA as well as values from the Glasgow Coma Scale are useful in classifying the severity of the trauma. Table 3.1 suggests guidelines for classifying TBI severity (Williamson, Scott, & Adams, 1996).

Cognitive and behavioral–personality sequelae of TBI are consistent with the areas of neuropathology noted above. Following moderate to severe TBI, deficits most commonly seen initially are in learning and long-term memory, higher level attention (e.g., divided attention, vigilance), cognitive flexibility, abstract reasoning, and planning. Slowing and decreased efficiency in information processing also exist. Deficits in learning and memory as well as the problems in higher order cognition are usually the most long-standing sequelae of moderate or severe TBI, even remaining for years after the injury occurs.

Emotional or behavioral consequences of TBI can be devastating for the patient and difficult for the family to accept. TBI survivors often manifest poor impulse control, social inappropriateness, poor planning and judgment, and deficient

Table 3.1

Traumatic Brain Injury Severity Classification

Indicator	Severity		
	Mild	Moderate	Severe
Duration of loss of consciousness	20 m or less	20 m–36 h	More than 36 h
Glasgow Coma Scale score	13–15	9–12	8 or less
Posttraumatic amnesia	Less than 24 h	1–7 days	More than 7 days

self-monitoring. Others display difficulties in initiation of behavior; they exhibit an akinetic syndrome, in which they seldom engage in spontaneous behavior. Family members often describe such patients as seeming like "a bump on a log."

Vascular Disorders

The vascular system affords the brain a continuous supply of oxygen and glucose and removes heat and metabolic debris. A variety of vascular conditions can dramatically affect central nervous system (CNS) functioning. The most common forms of cerebrovascular disorders are ischemic stroke, hemorrhagic stroke, arteriovenous malformations, and aneurysms.

The brain's vascular supply is generated by the carotid and vertebral arteries, which are positioned bilaterally below the base of the brain. The carotid artery divides to form the anterior cerebral artery (ACA) and middle cerebral artery (MCA) within each hemisphere of the brain; the vertebral artery ultimately forms each posterior cerebral artery (PCA). The circle of Willis, an intersection of the major arteries of the brain, provides contiguous circulation within the system.

Ischemic processes are divided into two major groups: thrombosis and embolism. Each of these conditions produces an insufficient supply of blood to the brain. In *thrombosis*, a blockage of blood, fat, or other substance coagulates and remains in the area in which it initially formed. An *embolism* is a clot that originates at one point in the vascular system but is transported to a smaller vascular area where it ultimately becomes lodged and creates a blockage. Although a major disruption of blood flow through a primary vessel produces immediate and dramatic neurological symptoms, transient involvement of a secondary vessel, known as a *transient ischemic attack*, produces less obvious or enduring symptoms.

Formation of atherosclerosis, or plaques composed of cholesterol, on the interior of the arteries leads to stenosis, a narrowing that occludes blood flow and can result in stroke. Atherosclerosis, hypertension, and aging are the most powerful predictors of stroke. Other evidence suggests that men and African Americans are at greater risk for stroke than are women and White people. Smoking and the use of birth control pills also are linked with higher risk for stroke.

When a blockage occurs, the cerebrovascular system might provide blood via an alternate route to the affected area of the brain following a stroke; however, a complete lack of blood flow to an area for a period of more than a few minutes results in neural damage. Along with the availability of a collateral blood supply to a given brain region, the relative metabolic demand of a neural substrate also influences the degree of neural damage sustained following a cardiovascular accident.

Approximately 250,000 individuals in the United States have strokes each year. Of those who have strokes, approximately 30%–50% die immediately or within several months of their strokes. About half of patients who survive require institutional or nursing care because of significant disability (Wiederholt, 1982).

Areas of the cortex or subcortex may undergo cerebrovascular events, but the MCA is the most frequent area of stroke. The MCA provides blood to an extensive area of the cortex that subserves motor and sensory functions for the contralateral side of the body (particularly related to the upper extremity and facial regions). The hemisphere that is affected generally dictates the types of symptoms seen. For example, an MCA stroke of the dominant hemisphere frequently results in language dysfunction and a specific aphasic syndrome. Nondominant (usually right) hemisphere strokes often result in an inattention syndrome in which the individual ignores or neglects stimuli presented to the contralateral side of the body. Individuals also may demonstrate *anosagnosia*— a lack of awareness of the disorder or symptoms they manifest.

Strokes of the ACA or PCA are less common than MCA strokes but produce characteristic symptom patterns as well.

ACA strokes result in weakness of the lower extremities and some sensory decline contralaterally. Cognitive decline and depressive symptomology also are common. The neuropsychological consequences of these strokes include impaired executive control functions, such as planning or initiation behaviors, and minimal interaction of the patient with his or her immediate environment. PCA strokes can result in memory impairment and contralateral or bilateral field cuts (an area of visual loss). When the dominant hemisphere is involved, deficits related to symbolic understanding (e.g., reading) may result as well.

Cerebrovascular disease also occurs subcortically. Some patients may not manifest obvious clinical syndromes characteristic of ischemic events yet have cumulative decline in cognitive and motor function as a result of multiple, small subcortical infarcts. These events may lead to specific deficits in the domains of language, memory, and motor functioning but can also produce a more diffuse dementia syndrome as well.

Hemorrhagic stroke, or *cerebral hemorrhage,* occurs when a breach of the cerebral vessels results in massive bleeding into the substance of the brain and is often fatal. High blood pressure or congenital defects in the integrity of the vessel wall can predate the apparently sudden onset of hemorrhage. Complications related to cerebral hemorrhage are due to increased pressure created by the presence of blood within the brain space and the toxic consequences of blood coming into direct contact with neural tissue.

Arteriovenous malformations are collections of irregular, enlarged, or tortuous cerebral vessels that create dysfunctional blood flow patterns within the brain. Such abnormal blood flow results in greater likelihood of ischemic events or in chronically deficient distribution of blood to specific cortical regions.

Aneurysms are enlarged areas of the cerebrovascular system secondary to defects in the composition of the walls of the vessel. Such abnormalities ultimately can rupture and produce immediate neurological impairment.

Dementia

The term *dementia* is used to identify a category of brain diseases that produce a chronic, slow deterioration of intellectual and adaptive functions (Strub & Black, 1988). These diseases have primarily cortical or subcortical neuropathologic effects. Although this family of disorders can affect people younger than age 65, the incidence rate of many dementia conditions increases with age. Some estimates suggest that more than half the population older than 90 meet criteria for a diagnosis of dementia. Incidence of dementia likely will continue to rise as life expectancy increases.

Dementia is reversible in some situations and results in diverse cognitive and functional deficits across subtypes and individuals. In addition, the course and progression of dementia vary widely. In this chapter I focus on four common subtypes of dementing illness: Alzheimer's disease, vascular dementia, Pick's disease, and Parkinson's disease.

Alzheimer's Disease

Alzheimer's disease, which has an insidious onset and a gradually progressive course of deterioration, is the cause of 65% or more of dementia cases. Fewer than 3 million cases were present in 1980, but U.S. Bureau of the Census projections indicate that 10.3 million U.S. citizens will have Alzheimer's disease by the year 2050 (Evans, 1990). Onset of Alzheimer's disease occurs after age 40 in 96% of the cases (Lechtenberg, 1982). Earlier onset of symptoms is associated with more severe and rapid courses of the disease (Lezak, 1983). Specific criteria relevant to a diagnosis of probable or possible Alzheimer's disease are presented in Exhibit 3.1.

The etiology of Alzheimer's disease is not completely understood but appears to possess a genetic component: Forty-three percent of monozygotic twins are concordant for the disorder, compared to 8% of dizygotic twins (Lishman, 1978).

Exhibit 3.1

Criteria for Diagnosis of Probable and Possible Alzheimer's Disease (AD)

Probable AD

Diagnostic criteria
1 Dementia established by clinical examination, mental status testing, and neuropsychological assessment.
2 Deficits into more areas of cognition.
3 Progressive worsening of memory and other cognitive functions.
4 No disturbance of consciousness.
5 Onset between the ages of 40 and 90 years, usually after age 65.
6 Absence of systemic disorders or other brain disease that could account for the decline in memory and cognitive function.

Additional findings that support the diagnosis
1 Progressive deterioration of cognitive functions, such as language, motor skills, and perception.
2 Impaired activities of daily living and altered patterns of behavior.
3 Family history of similar disorders.
4 Any of the following laboratory findings
  a. Normal lumbar puncture.
  b. Normal pattern or nonspecific changes in EEG, such as increased slow-wave activity.
  c. Evidence of cerebral atrophy on CT that is progressive on serial observation.

Other findings consistent with the diagnosis
1 Plateaus in the progression of symptoms.
2 Associated symptoms of depression; insomnia; incontinence; delusions; illusions; hallucinations; catastrophic verbal, emotional, or physical outbursts; sexual disorders; and weight loss.
3 Neurological abnormalities, including motor signs, such as increased muscle tone, myoclonus, or gait disorder, especially in more advanced disease.
4 Seizures in advanced disease.
5 CT normal for age.

Exhibit 3.1 *Continued*

Clinical features that make the diagnosis uncertain or unlikely
1   Sudden, apoplectic onset.
2   Focal neurological findings such as hemiparesis, sensory loss, visual field deficits, and incoordination early in the course of the illness.
3   Seizures or gait disturbance at the onset or very early in course of illness.

Possible AD

A diagnosis of possible AD may be made when
1   There is evidence of dementia with atypical presentation or course, in the absence of other neurological, psychiatric, or systematic disorders sufficient to cause dementia.
2   A second systemic or brain disorder is present that might produce dementia but that is not considered the sole cause of cognitive impairment.
3   There is a single, severe cognitive deficit that is gradually progressive and does not have a specific identified cause.

Note. EEG = electroencephalogram; CT = computerized tomography. From "Clinical diagnosis of Alzheimer's disease," by G. McKhann, D. Drachman, M. Folstein, R. Katzman, D. Price, and E. M. Stadlan, 1984, *Neurology,* 34, p. 940. Copyright 1984 by Lippincott Williams & Wilkins. Adapted by permission of the publisher.

Some investigations have targeted genetic factors and suggest that being homozygous for the apolipoprotein E-4 allele is predictive of later incidence. Etiologies related to environmental exposures or nutritional deficiencies also have been explored.

Although the neuropathology of Alzheimer's disease is mysterious, several pathophysiological processes (e.g., neurofibrillary tangles, an abnormality of the cytoplasm of the neurons within the cerebral cortex; senile plaques, extracellular abnormalities involving the accumulation of amyloid [a starchy substance]; Hirano bodies, rodlike structures found in the hippocampus of patients who have Alzheimer's disease) have been observed in analysis of brain tissue from Alzheimer's disease patients. A significant loss of nerve cells and dendritic spines and shrinkage of existing neurons accompany these markers. The atrophy often visualized on computerized tomography (CT) scans may be more related to the dendritic loss and shrinkage than to simple neuron loss alone (Wolf, 1980). Gross neuropathology during the initial stages of the disease is most prominent in the temporal and parietal regions, with an accompanying sparing of the sensory and motor cortexes.

Neurocognitive features of the disease include deficits in the consolidation and storage of new memories and a rapid rate of forgetting of newly acquired information. Also, impairment of executive control functions and difficulty with confrontational naming (orally identifying objects presented visually) emerge early in the course of the illness. As the disease progresses, global cognitive decline occurs, and overall intellectual deficits, frank aphasia, apraxia (disturbance of purposeful movement), and agnosia (disturbance of object recognition) often emerge. These difficulties, along with pronounced deficiencies in reasoning and problem solving, take a dramatic toll on functional abilities. Thus, even long-standing and well-rehearsed activities, such as paying bills, driving a car, and cooking meals, become impossible for the patient to negotiate or represent too great a safety risk to be carried out independently.

Neurobehavioral aspects of Alzheimer's disease include alterations in personality style, such as apathy or social withdrawal; increased fatigability; and disinhibition and lack of socially appropriate behavior. Psychological symptoms include mild to moderate depression or increased emotional lability. More significant psychopathology manifests during the late stages of the disease and can include sleep and appetite disturbance; increased motor restlessness and wandering; and development of delusions, which may be the result of perceptual distortions and generalized confusion.

Vascular Dementia

Multiple small cerebrovascular accidents can result in a *vascular dementia*, which is characterized by rapid onset with a stepwise pattern of further deterioration. Whereas patients who have Alzheimer's disease display a slow and gradual pattern of cognitive decline, an individual manifesting a vascular dementia demonstrates a rapid decline of cognition, which may be followed by alternating periods of relatively stable functioning and further rapid decline. The Hachinski Ischemic Scale (see Table 3.2) summarizes and quantifies for diagnostic purposes information concerning symptom onset, disease course, and the patient's previous vascular history (Hachinski, 1983). Scores for each indicator are summed and form the total ischemic score. For diagnostic purposes, scores $\geq$ suggest vascular etiologies, whereas scores $\leq$ point to nonvascular dementia.

It is estimated that 15%–25% of all cases of dementia have etiologies related to cerebrovascular disease (Snyder & Nussbaum, 1998). Whereas onset and symptom progression usually are rapid following an extensive infarct, clinical presentation is more insidious in cases of small-vessel, subcortical disease. Factors increasing the risk of vascular dementia in-

Table 3.2

Revised Ischemic Score

Clinical indicator	Score
Abrupt onset	2
Stepwise deterioration	1
Somatic complaints	1
Emotional incontinence	1
History of hypertension	1
History of strokes	2
Focal neurological symptoms	2
Focal neurological signs	2

clude a history of hypertension, tobacco use, age, diabetes, and obesity.

In neuropsychological terms, a *symptom constellation* is described as focal, multifocal, or "patchy" and corresponds to the site of the vascular lesion(s). Lateralized motor or sensory deficits, language impairments, or modality-specific memory decline are common.

Small-vessel disease within the subcortical regions of the brain often signals a lacunar stroke, in which the subcortical tissue is damaged by small, pitted lesions. In clinical terms, this group may present with apathy, lack of motivation, and akinetic mutism, with preserved insight and personality style (Ishii, Nishihara, & Imamura, 1986). It is not uncommon, however, for these individuals to present with a pseudobulbar state in which they manifest prolonged episodes of spontaneous laughing or crying that are unrelated to events or situations in the patient's environment.

Pick's Disease

Similar to Alzheimer's disease in its status as an untreatable degenerative dementia, Pick's disease is typically differentiated from Alzheimer's disease on the basis of histological findings. On microscopic examination, the cortex displays cell loss, astrocytic gliosis, and many enlarged balloon-shaped cells known as *Pick's cells*. In general, the outer layers of the cortex have more neuropathology. Although primary projection areas (areas that first process incoming sensory information) of the cortex are spared, the association cortex in the frontal and temporal regions is often involved.

Clinical presentation of the disease is dependent on whether the patient has primarily frontal lobe atrophy or mostly temporal or frontotemporal atrophy (Constantinidis, 1985). Individuals in the primarily frontal subgroup often display dramatic alterations in personality and social behavior rather than initial impairments of memory or cognition. Following deficits in social interaction and loss of social inhibitions, a more pervasive lack of interest in social and vocational pursuits occurs. In keeping with this lack of awareness or insight is an absence of insight concerning the disease. Cognitive functions are less impaired in the early stages of the disease but emerge later and commonly affect the domains of language and speech production. Specific language difficulties manifest as reduced speech production, anomia (word-finding problems), the presence of stereotyped language, or a perseverative quality to speech.

Patients who sustain temporal or frontotemporal atrophy demonstrate earlier declines in memory with accompanying affective changes and the presence of childish behavior (Constantinidis, 1985). Although symptom presentation in the early and middle stages of the disease is different from that of Alzheimer's disease, Pick's disease becomes more similar to Alzheimer's disease during the final stage, as pervasive dementia is characteristic (Strub & Black, 1988).

Parkinson's Disease

Unlike Alzheimer's disease and Pick's disease, which primarily produce cortical atrophy and higher order cognitive and behavioral changes, Parkinson's disease is strongly subcortical in nature. Given the impact of subcortical regions on motor behavior, the most salient symptoms accompanying the disease include bradykinesia (slowness of movement), a resting tremor, and rigidity. Although James Parkinson identified no cognitive deficits in the disease now named after him, approximately 50% of patients with Parkinson's disease evidence dementia (Lechtenberg, 1982). In addition, as many as 90% of patients show mild neuropsychological deficits when examined with appropriately sensitive cognitive measures (Cummings, 1985).

Parkinson's disease typically affects individuals older than age 50 and is slightly more common in men than in women. Parkinsonism is the clinical expression of dysregulation of the dopaminergic neurotransmitter system, which is involved in motor and purposeful behavior. This deficiency is most related to the neuronal loss within a specific region of the substantia nigra. Other pathology associated with the disease includes neuronal loss in the basilar nucleus of Meynert

(Whitehouse, Hedreen, White, & Price, 1983) and existence of abnormal formations known as *Lewy bodies* in parts of the brain, including the midbrain (Gibb, 1992). Many patients also evidence basal ganglia changes (Olanow, 1992).

Patients with Parkinson's disease often exhibit a diffuse and pervasive degree of cognitive slowing (bradyphrenia), which results in general declines in cognitive efficiency. Patients often manifest deficits within the domains of problem solving and concept formation. Insight and judgment may dramatically decline, and social role performance may be impaired because of episodes of impulsive or inappropriate behavior. Neuropsychological testing can reveal deficits in verbal memory for tasks involving free recall of novel information (Soukup & Adams, 1996). People with Parkinson's disease also exhibit difficulty with constructional tasks, verbal fluency, nonverbal reasoning, and certain aspects of speech perception (Strub & Black, 1988). The existence of depression in many Parkinsonian patients makes it more difficult to acquire an accurate assessment of cognitive status. A recent investigation suggests a 47% prevalence of depression in this group (Dooneief et al., 1992).

Treatment for Parkinson's disease consists of Levadopa therapy aimed at reducing the debilitating motor symptoms. The effectiveness of this pharmacologic agent may wane over time, but it usually proves beneficial during the first several years of treatment. Neurosurgical treatment targets the underlying dopamine deficiency or corrects abnormal compensatory effects in neural circuits of the basal ganglia (Soukup & Adams, 1996).

Epilepsy

Epilepsy occurs in approximately 5 of every 1,000 children (Cowan, Bodensteider, Leviton, & Doherty, 1989) and in 4–7 of every 1,000 adults (Hauser & Annegers, 1993). Incidence rates are highest in infants, young children, and elderly people (Brown et al., 1993). Although some seizures are the result of a specific neurological insult, the majority of seizures may be idiopathic in nature with no clear etiology. Indeed, Lishman (1987) posited that an unknown etiology accounts for as many as two thirds of all seizure cases.

The causes of epilepsy are numerous, and many etiologies are poorly understood. Heritability can involve either the general tendency toward lowered seizure threshold or a specific condition associated with epilepsy (Anderson & Hauser, 1993). Conditions related to complications of birth may result in neurological damage that is later the impetus for seizure activity. Early infections or metabolic or cardiac conditions can produce seizures. Incidence of hypoxia (reduced oxygen to the brain) also may produce scarring of brain tissue that later spawns abnormal brain activity. Causes of epilepsy in adults include trauma, vascular disease, degenerative disease, and withdrawal from alcohol or other substances. Although seizures may originate from most areas of the cortex or subcortex, many such disorders have an onset within the temporal cortex. Neurochemically, seizures result from deficiencies of the inhibitory neurotransmitter gamma-aminobutyric acid (GABA). Reduced GABA levels result in excessive excitation at the cellular level (Adams & Victor, 1993). It is the GABA system that is targeted with many anticonvulsant medications, which facilitate the inhibitory process by increasing GABA levels (Stevenson & King, 1987).

Seizures are commonly classified as *partial* or *generalized*. Onset of partial seizures is local in nature (e.g., left temporal lobe). Partial seizures are either simple or complex. A simple seizure does not produce loss of consciousness; a complex seizure impairs consciousness. Generalized seizures have bilateral, or symmetrical, onset and fall broadly into one of two classes: generalized convulsive seizures and absence seizures. Convulsive seizures are further classified by the specific nature of abnormal muscle activity, which accompanies the seizure. Absence seizures are marked by the absence of gross muscular convulsions and other symptoms seen in convulsive seizures. However, they produce lapses in attention and accompanying blinking of the eyes or upward rotation of the eyes.

There is no universal cognitive profile in epilepsy. However, the Neuropsychological Battery for Epilepsy (Dodrill, 1978) is sensitive to the detection of cognitive deficits related to electroencephalogram epileptiform abnormalities. Along with the tests that make up the Halstead–Reitan Battery, the Neuropsychological Battery for Epilepsy includes the Stroop Test (Stroop, 1935) and elements from the Wechsler Memory Scale (Wechsler, 1997b). The most important aspect of the assessment process with an epileptic patient is the inclusion of a clinical interview that reviews clinical problems in a precise manner.

Neoplasm

Neoplasms, or tumors, of the CNS are categorized as primary or metastatic. Primary tumors arise directly from cells of the nervous system or elements that intimately support the brain or spinal cord, such as the cerebrovasculature or the meningeal coverings. Metastatic lesions initially emerge in some other area of the body (e.g., lung, gastrointestinal system) and subsequently infiltrate the CNS. Understanding of the etiology of many types of brain tumors is limited. Although heredity, virus, previous trauma, and radiation exposure all have been offered as putative causes of CNS neoplastic disease, there is little direct evidence to support universally these hypotheses.

Like cerebrovascular conditions, tumors of the brain often produce some focal symptomology. Unlike the specific neurobehavioral syndromes that follow many types of vascular events, neoplastic lesions also may produce more general impairments, such as confusion, secondary to edema (swelling) and rises in intracranial pressure. Several characteristics of the tumor dictate the magnitude and nature of subsequent neuropsychological and behavioral sequelae produced by the lesion. Type of tumor, velocity of growth, location of tumor, and age of onset are factors that determine the overall symptom pattern and degree of functional impairment experienced by the patient.

Tumors are either *intrinsic* (arising from cells within the brain) or *extrinsic* (arising from cells or tissue outside the brain). Intrinsic tumors are more likely to produce edema and subsequent increases of intracranial pressure. The rise in intracranial pressure can lead to herniation of the brain through cranial openings. This situation often affects lower brain structures, such as the pons or midbrain, but also can affect cranial structures, particularly on the inferior surface of the brain. Some neoplasms of the CNS can be classified as benign or malignant, although this distinction is less clear when describing brain or spinal tumors than when describing tumors outside the CNS. Also, this distinction can be misleading when discussing tumors of the CNS, because even benign tumors can be lethal when they compress brain structures that are critical to the maintenance of life-sustaining functions.

The growth characteristics of a tumor are important in determining the effect the lesion will have on the patient's presentation and degree of functional impairment. Slow-growing tumors may allow healthy brain tissue a greater opportunity to accommodate the lesion, resulting in a greater level of compensation by the patient. For this reason, slowly developing neoplasms may receive delayed medical attention because of a lack of alerting signs or symptoms. Symptoms in such cases may represent general, and at times mild, cognitive decline rather than focal neuropsychological deficits in a specific domain, such as language or spatial abilities. Faster growing tumors or those producing greater swelling of surrounding tissue frequently are accompanied by more specific neurological or psychiatric manifestations.

The nature of the clinical presentation also is influenced by the location of the neoplasm. Individuals presenting with primarily psychiatric symptoms usually have tumor loci near frontal or temporal limbic structures (Malmud, 1967). Because nearly 50% of all patients with brain tumors demonstrate some psychiatric symptoms, such patients may initially seek a psychologist rather than a neurologist. Other symptoms predominate regardless of localizing features. For example, headache is one of the most common physical complaints and occurs as the initial symptom in approximately

20% of cases (Reitan & Wolfson, 1992). Dizziness, vomiting, and seizure episodes occur with relatively high frequency as well. Table 3.3 contains a summary of elements that are critically associated with brain tumors and should be considered when gathering a patient's clinical history (Strub & Black, 1988).

Indicators listed in Table 3.3 are clinically relevant yet not unique to neoplastic diseases of the brain and thus cannot be used alone for diagnostic, prognostic, or treatment purposes. Along with thorough neurological investigation, neuroradiological procedures, such as CT or magnetic resonance imaging technologies, are often the most definitive diagnostic

Table 3.3

Indicators of Potential Brain Tumor Within the Clinical History

Indicator	Nature of indicator
Headache	Often one of the earliest symptoms of neoplastic disease of the brain. Often appears worse on awakening in the morning and at night.
Epileptic seizures	Common alerting sign of brain tumor in an adult. Seizure activity is particularly common with temporal lobe lesions.
History of a previous cancer diagnosis	Metastatic tumors affecting the central nervous system most often arise from primary cancer of the lung or breast.
Nausea or vomiting	Can worsen in the morning.
Visual disturbance	Diminished visual accuity, blurring, or perceptual deficits become more noticeable as intracranial pressure increases in response to tumor growth.
Focal neurological symptoms	Specific sensory or motor deficits or disturbances of cranial nerve functions indicate a potential brain tumor.
Various neurobehavioral manifestations	General cognitive or behavioral changes occur relatively frequently. Increased fatigability, drowsiness, and altered consciousness are also seen.

methods when a brain tumor is suspected. Treatment of CNS tumors is typically approached through surgery, chemotherapy, or radiation. Psychologists or neuropsychologists who work with individuals coping with neoplastic disease should be aware that each of these treatment modalities can have deleterious effects on cognitive functioning. Thus, comprehensive psychological and neuropsychological assessment may be necessary even after diagnosis and treatment of the disorder are accomplished.

Infectious Conditions

A complete discussion of all forms of infectious processes that may involve the CNS is outside the scope of this book. Instead, I will focus my discussion on examples of general infectious conditions that are more likely to be encountered in clinical practice or those that often present with behavioral or psychological changes.

Meningitis

Meningitis is a disorder related to bacterial or viral infection of the cerebrospinal fluid that results in inflammation of the meninges. Prior to the advent of antibiotics, meningitis was often fatal; however, antibiotics and recent improvements in diagnostic methods have significantly lowered the mortality rate in cases of meningitis. General signs that accompany meningitis include headache, stiff neck, and fever. The clinician may witness few focal symptoms and instead observe general behavioral effects, such as altered levels of consciousness, lethargy, and confusion. Aggressive bacteria produce an acute inflammatory process that can rapidly impinge on the ventricular system, causing constriction and reduced ventricular flow that culminates in increased intracranial pressure. Because of the importance of rapid diagnosis and treatment, a clinician who sees any evidence of meningitis in a client should make an immediate medical referral.

Brain Abscess

Brain abscesses are typically conveyed from the frontal sinus or the middle ear and present as a focal space-occupying lesion. The effect on the brain of the lesion produces a greater risk to the patient than the infection itself. Because increased cranial pressure results in symptoms such as vomiting, headache, and generalized cognitive decline, many brain abscesses are initially suspected to be neoplastic. Although brain abscesses can evolve in any brain region, they are disproportionately found in cortical rather than subcortical structures, often in frontal and inferior temporal regions, specifically. Given the focal nature of brain abscesses, specific neuropsychological syndromes, such as aphasic or agraphic disturbance, follow intrusion into the dominant hemisphere. Treatment of the abscess may consist of aggressive antibiotic intervention and surgical aspiration of the infectious brain mass.

Encephalitis

Encephalitis refers to the inflammatory process that results from the invasion of brain tissue by a variety of infectious agents. Although the process often produces widespread CNS consequences and diffuse impairment of mentation, some forms of encephalitis may result in specific behavioral or neuropsychological symptoms. A common form of viral encephalitis associated with specific neurobehavioral consequences of a residual nature is *herpes simplex*. Along with the initial general medical symptoms (e.g., headache, fever), herpes simplex can produce either an acute delirium or confusional state as well as focal neuropsychological syndromes, including language deficits, memory decline, or psychological changes. The neuropathologic changes that accompany herpes simplex have an affinity for certain limbic structures, such as the hippocampus. This selectivity for hippocampal tissue is a likely factor in producing the nearly comprehensive memory deficits that are a hallmark of the residual cognitive sequelae. The virus is transmitted along the trigeminal cranial nerve and can lay dormant in the brain until it is activated at a later time.

Metabolic Conditions or Endocrine Disorders

Many potentially reversible metabolic conditions or endocrine disorders can lead to acute or gradual mental status changes and neurobehavioral symptoms. Symptom patterns of these disorders are discussed next.

The endocrine disorders *hyperthyroidism* and *hypothyroidism* (overactivity and underactivity of the thyroid gland, respectively) can produce dramatic affective, cognitive, and behavioral alterations. Some hyperthyroid patients display a characteristic hyperactivity or agitation; others exhibit affective elements that are more typical of depressive illness. Individuals who have hypothyroidism often demonstrate decreased intellectual functioning and elements of cognitive and/or motor slowing. This symptom picture can emerge gradually and at times resemble the progressive decline often associated with dementia. The distinction is critical, however, as thyroid conditions are often treatable once they are diagnosed. Dysfunction of the pituitary or adrenal system also can produce acute or gradual mental status deficits and psychological symptoms.

Metabolic deficiencies or disorders of specific bodily organs also can result in direct or indirect neuropathologic changes that may lead to cognitive and intellectual dysfunction. One such condition is *Wilson's disease*, in which a rare disorder of copper metabolism causes copper ions to remain in the liver and in some subcortical regions of the brain. Because of the subcortical pathology of the disorder, many of the early neurological symptoms are motoric and often include tremor, rigidity, and dysarthria (motor speech impairment). When a behavioral or psychological component exists with the condition, it often includes emotional lability; silly, immature, or impulsive behavior; and sexual promiscuity (Strub & Black, 1988). Many patients also demonstrate decreased memory and attentional and higher order cognitive difficulties (e.g., judgment, reasoning).

Hypoxia, or the reduced availability of oxygen to the brain, is a broad neuropathologic category that may be brought on by different traumatic or medical circumstances. Cardiac failure, restricted circulatory functioning, and respiratory arrest can produce hypoxia, or even anoxia—a complete loss of oxygen to the brain. Situations that can lead to hypoxic states include carbon monoxide poisoning, smoke inhalation, electrocution, and strangulation. Given the neuron's inability to store oxygen for later use, brain cells are destroyed within approximately 5 min when anoxia is complete, resulting in permanent injury or brain death. Hypoxia may produce deficits of attention, memory, or judgment.

Another endocrine condition that may present with largely behavioral or psychiatric disturbance is hypoglycemia (low blood sugar). Because glucose is a nutritional staple of the CNS, even temporary deficiencies in the brain's available supply of glucose may result in neurological complications. Hypoglycemia is not a specific disease process; it results from situations that lead to reduced blood sugar. When these situations occur, the sympathetic nervous system responds with symptoms of hypertension, tachycardia, sweating, and malaise. Cognitive or emotional features may include only irritability or anxiety, or they may include more dramatic symptoms, such as disorientation, confusion, suspiciousness, and hallucinatory experiences. In the most severe cases, individuals experience loss of consciousness or coma. The reversibility of an acute hypoglycemic episode is startling once correctly identified and appropriately treated with intravenous glucose. Cases have been reported in which individuals who were incoherent and confused and exhibiting psychotic characteristics became cogent and manageable within minutes following the administration of glucose.

Conclusion

Issues related to initial diagnosis of neurological impairment may be handled by treating physicians, neurologists, and neuropsychologists, but management and treatment of "organic" conditions is often left to the psychologist. Anticipating the broad array of emotional and psychosocial difficulties that often plague clients with neurological involvement may greatly enhance treatment planning and eventual outcome of psychotherapeutic interventions. Awareness of the specific cognitive deficits that accompany many neurobehavioral syndromes can assist in expediting and focusing the delivery of psychological services that are better tailored to the unique needs of the cognitively involved client. This last consideration is especially relevant given the increasing economical demands of a service delivery affected by the constraints of a managed-care environment.

Additional Reading

Neurobehavioral Disorders: A Clinical Approach (Strub & Black, 1988), *Clinical Syndromes in Adult Neuropsychology: The Practitioner's Handbook* (White, 1992), and *Neuropsychological Assessment of Neuropsychiatric Disorders* (2nd ed., Grant & Adams, 1996) offer background regarding the neuropsychological sequelae of specific neurological or psychiatric conditions.

Chapter

4

Relation Between Non-Neurological Elements and Cognitive Functioning

When general clinicians encounter clients who have impaired neuropsychological functioning, it is important to know that such impairment may or may not be the result of actual neurological insult. Developmental and psychological factors and conditions are complexly interrelated with cognitive functioning and the manner in which psychotherapeutic, case management, rehabilitation, and family assistance services are delivered. Developmental and psychological conditions, such as learning disability (LD) and depression, can produce neuropsychological impairment; likewise, neurological and other medical conditions can produce psychological symptoms that in turn affect neuropsychological performance. Accordingly, if a client exhibits deficits in neuropsychological functioning, those deficits could be the result of a developmental or psychological condition, the result of a psychological condition that occurs in response to neurological insult (or perceived neurological insult), or, as might be assumed, the result of neurological insult itself.

Obviously, differential diagnosis is challenging when the influences of developmental, psychological, or psychosocial factors become entangled with the effects of neuropathology on cognitive performance. In such cases, the general clinician can benefit from referring the client for a neuropsychological consultation to clarify the extent of neuropsychological involvement rather than simplistically placing the client into either the "organic" (biological) or the "functional" (behavioral) diagnostic group. The neuropsychologist is faced with the task of apportioning the relative contributions of neurological and psychological factors. A statement from the therapist to the neuropsychologist concerning the nature, severity, and duration of existing psychological disorders can assist the specialist in estimating the contributions of psychological and neurological influences on neuropsychological examination findings.

Moreover, cognizance of the etiology and nature of the developmental, psychological, and psychosocial consequences generated by neurological conditions is necessary in the long-term management and treatment of such conditions. The psychological and psychosocial aspects of head injury, for example, are critical in predicting which individuals will successfully return to various social and occupational roles. In addition, patients who experience physiological conditions with accompanying psychological and behavioral repercussions may recover from the physiological symptoms but retain psychological and behavioral changes that need to be addressed by a general clinician.

When making an appropriate referral and integrating the findings of subsequent neuropsychological evaluation into the general assessment and treatment plan, therefore, it is crucial to understand the relation between non-neurological elements and neuropsychological impairment. These constructs should be viewed as overlapping or additive rather than as mutually exclusive. A richer comprehension of the relation may be facilitated by placing the complex non-neurological factors that influence neuropsychological performance along a continuum rather than into restrictive categories such as organic or functional. Figure 4.1 is an illustration of this concept.

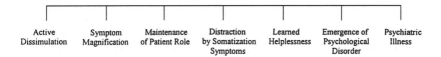

| Active Dissimulation | Symptom Magnification | Maintenance of Patient Role | Distraction by Somatization Symptoms | Learned Helplessness | Emergence of Psychological Disorder | Psychiatric Illness |

Figure 4.1. Continuum of factors that affect neuropsychological performance.

Developmental Factors and Conditions

Traditionally, developmental conditions such as attention-deficit/hyperactivity disorder (ADHD) and LD have been considered non-neurological in nature, yet neuropsychological testing of individuals with these conditions shows impairment. Evidence now exists that ADHD and LD are associated with specific patterns of neuropsychological deficit and underlying neuropathologic correlates.

Attention-deficit Hyperactivity Disorder

Initially viewed as a psychiatric condition of childhood, ADHD is now recognized to persist often into adulthood. Estimates of the prevalence of ADHD in the adult population are conflicting, although Wender (1995) assessed the figure as ranging from 2% to 7%. Some adults with ADHD readily note their attentional difficulties; many do not, and clinicians must carefully observe behavior to obtain the information.

Etiologically speaking, ADHD has a strong genetic transmission that is perhaps related to a dominant major gene rather than to genetic heterogeneity or polygeneticism (Wender, 1995). At a neurochemical level, both the dopaminergic and noradrenergic systems are critically related to ADHD (Oades, 1987). Although a variety of neuroanatomic substrates have been posited as important to the development of ADHD symptoms, the frontal lobes are crucial. Denckla (1991) identified structures within the limbic system and basal ganglia, along with the frontal lobes, as responsible for the functional elements of attention and pointed to four actions that underlie attentional capacity: initiate, sustain, inhibit, shift. These constructs are frontally mediated and thus tapped by executive control tasks. Additional evidence supporting a frontal lobe dysfunction explanation for ADHD comes from neuropsychological studies of children and adults with ADHD. Chelune, Ferguson, Koon, and Dickey (1986) conducted one of the first such investigations, which revealed a greater degree of persevering errors and fewer categories on the Wisconsin Card Sorting Test—a task that requires abstract reasoning and problem solving. Although some executive control measures that tap vigilance and susceptibility to interference are sensitive to ADHD, Barkley, Grodzinsky, and DuPaul (1992) indicated that some frontal lobe instruments may not reliably reveal the disorder.

ADHD is divided into two symptom groups: inattention and hyperactivity–impulsivity. On the basis of symptoms characteristic of these two groups, the *Diagnostic and Statistical Manual of Mental Disorders* (4th ed.; *DSM–IV*; American Psychiatric Association, 1994) classifies ADHD into these subtypes:

□   Attention-Deficit/Hyperactivity Disorder, Predominantly Inattentive Type
□   Attention-Deficit/Hyperactivity Disorder, Predominantly Hyperactive–Impulsive Type
□   Attention-Deficit/Hyperactivity Disorder, Combined Type.

The general clinician's initial evaluation should help determine the required breadth of subsequent neuropsychological assessment. It will determine whether neuropsychological assessment should be aimed at only attentional difficulties or whether a broader evaluation is needed.

A general practitioner who is conducting a clinical interview with a client who potentially has ADHD should look for the presence of primary ADHD symptoms, pervasiveness of such symptoms, and evidence of comorbid disorders. ADHD symptoms in adults characteristically reflect, rather than manifest as, inattention, hyperactivity or motor abnormalities, and impulsivity. In other words, adults with ADHD do not exhibit the dramatically excessive movements or constant running or climbing that are common in childhood cases. Instead, they may feel uncomfortable when sitting still or need to be active and find it difficult to relax. In adult ADHD, impulsivity represents the symptom set with the greatest potential for destructive psychosocial and vocational consequences. Episodes of impulsivity sometimes result in abrupt terminations of employment or severance of personal relationships. Distractibility and compromises of short-term memory also create vocational and interpersonal problems.

A clinical interview can be critical in uncovering comorbid conditions, such as LD, or determining that onset of attentional difficulties corresponded to a stressful life event (e.g., death of a sibling). A clinical interview should include questioning and formal rating scales that address symptoms of ADHD and symptom patterns that emerge developmentally. The clinical history should address academic, medical, developmental, and family history. Because ADHD, which can be genetically transmitted, was only recently identified as an adult disorder, asking adults if they have children who have been diagnosed with ADHD might be helpful. Questions surrounding psychological and behavioral milestones should be included.

Along with a comprehensive clinical interview and specific rating scales (Ward, Wender, & Reimherr, 1993), emotional and personality functioning should be addressed with an instrument that is relatively broad in psychological scope, such as the Minnesota Multiphasic Personality Inventory–2 or the Personality Assessment Inventory (Morey, 1991). General cognitive assessment and specific attentional testing should be included as well.

Learning Disability

A prevailing lack of clarity and consensus concerning a definition of what constitutes LD has hampered the study of it. Questions about the operational criteria for diagnosing LD have provoked concerns regarding the validity of diagnosis. Not unchallenged, a current working definition of LD requires that an individual must evidence average intellectual functioning coupled with subaverage academic achievement in at least one principal academic domain (e.g., reading, writing, spelling, arithmetic). Even the degree of discrepancy between IQ and achievement scores necessary to meet the criteria for LD is controversial—different states require discrepancies ranging from one to two standard deviations. In Table 4.1 are identified five components that generally emerge as consistent across various state classification systems (Chalfant, 1984).

In the same way that many adults continue to manifest attentional difficulties that first emerged during childhood, LD accompanies many individuals into adulthood (Culbertson & Edmonds, 1996). Gerber et al. (1990) asserted compellingly that LD actually worsens in adulthood. Approximately 4% of all school-age children manifest some form of LD (Chalfant, 1989); figures for the number of adults with

Table 4.1

Determinants in the Diagnosis of Learning Disability

Determinant	Description
IQ/achievement discrepancy	Difference between overall intellectual ability and achievement in one of the seven domains required by federal regulations
Failure in achievement	Lack of academic achievement in a specific domain (e.g., reading)
Exclusionary etiology	Factors in the medical and developmental history (e.g., delayed language acquisition, neurological diagnosis) used to determine the origins of specific learning difficulties
Psychological process disorders	Basic processes or cognitive capacities (e.g., attention, information processing) that underlie academic learning
Exclusionary factors	Symptoms that may be produced by unrelated conditions or circumstances (e.g., sensory deficit, educational or economic disadvantage)

LD are less clear. Hirshorn (1988) indicated that 1% of first-year college students report having some LD.

The subtypes of LD common among child clinical populations also are clinically relevant with adults. LD is a heterogeneous disorder with subtypes based on underlying neuropathology or clinical presentation. Verbal LDs are associated with dominant hemisphere involvement, and nonverbal LDs are associated with nondominant hemisphere involvement. The clinical utility of subtyping has merit in increasing knowledge about the pathological processes underlying the various subtypes, thereby assisting practitioners in focusing intervention.

In assessing the possibility of LD, general clinicians should gather a thorough developmental and academic history. This history, coupled with a review of pertinent school records, helps clinicians establish a pattern consistent with a "failure to achieve" in one or more of the principal academic domains. Reviewing the client's medical, developmental, and academic history also identifies etiologic factors that can later clarify an emerging pattern of deficits. During the record review and clinical interview, the general clinician should consider exclusionary variables that could masquerade as a formal LD. For example, basic sensory–perceptual deficits may account for a failure to achieve academically but might be excluded on the basis of a review of school- or medical-based visual and auditory screenings. Similarly, a review of the individual's emotional–psychological status and history can yield important information regarding the possibility that an emotional disorder predated evidence of LD. Finally, the history and interview can clarify the specific types of problems an individual has within a given academic domain. For example, written language difficulty might be characterized by slowness in thought formulation or in forming letters and words.

Formal testing should begin with a measure of cognitive ability such as the Wechsler Intelligence Scale for Children–III (Wechsler, 1991) and a relatively broad assessment of academic achievement, which can be provided by measures such as the Woodcock–Johnson Psychoeducational Battery–

Revised (Woodcock & Johnson, 1989) or the Wechsler Individual Achievement Test (Psychological Corporation, 1992). Kamphaus (1993) provided an informative review of common cognitive measures helpful in the assessment of learning disabilities.

With information generated by a review of pertinent medical and academic records, the clinical interview, and formal testing of general ability and academic achievement, general clinicians are in an informed position when referring patients for additional cognitive assessment. In addition, information gathered during the general clinician's evaluation is invaluable to the neuropsychologist in focusing his or her examination, thereby facilitating an efficient referral process.

Psychological Conditions, Factors, and States

The issue of the impact of psychological disturbance on cognitive assessment is unsettled because of limited empirical work examining the role psychological factors play in neuropsychological test performance. Also, no comprehensive examinations specifically evaluate the relation between depression severity and neuropsychological test performance (Caine, 1986; Finlayson & Bird, 1991). When interpreting data, some neuropsychologists de-emphasize the impact of psychological distress on the neuropsychological examination (Reitan & Wolfson, 1985), but most take into account the possible influences of psychological disturbance.

Certain psychological conditions, factors, or states are more prevalent than others in affecting neuropsychological performance. General clinicians can benefit from a working knowledge of the relation between such variables and cognitive functioning.

Emotional Disturbance

Affective disorders. Unipolar depression produces specific deficits in the domains of learning and memory (King, Caine,

& Cox, 1993; Speedie, Rabins, & Pearlson, 1990) and psycho-motor speed (Cassens, Wolfe, & Zola, 1990)—both areas that require effortful processing. Thus, effortful processing may be the activation component responsible for some of the per-formance impairment noted in patients who have depression. This possibility is further supported by the finding of better memory performance on recognition trials that eliminate the need for effortful recall strategies. Typically, such deficits in recall are seen in clients with levels of depression severe enough to require inpatient treatment. Fischer, Sweet, and Pfaelzer-Smith (1986) found depressed patients to be im-paired on 10 of 14 measures, suggesting a broader array of deficits. They recommend that clinicians adjust their impair-ment criteria when working with depressed patients to pre-vent diagnostic misclassification.

Little information is available concerning the cognitive impact of bipolar disturbance. In one study, neurologically intact patients with bipolar disorder showed impairment in the "focusing–executing domain" when assessed by tasks such as the Trail Making Test, the Stroop Color–Word In-terference Test, and the Purdue Pegboard Test; they did not, however, differ from the healthy control sample on tasks of learning or memory (Jones, Duncan, Mirsky, Post, & Theo-dore, 1994).

Anxiety disorders. Anxiety is another common psycholog-ical condition that affects neuropsychological performance. The majority of studies examining the impact of general anx-iety on cognitive test performance have found mild declines on tests of psychomotor speed, focused attention, and con-centration or vigilance (Hodges & Spielberger, 1969). Dodrill (1979) found significant anxiety effects related to gender for normal control participants but not for neurological patients. Posttraumatic stress disorder is also seen occasionally in pa-tients undergoing neuropsychological evaluation. Patients with posttraumatic stress disorder have particular difficulty on tasks that demand attentional processes or psychomotor speed.

Somatization and Hypochondriasis

Base rates of self-reported somatic symptoms are common in non-neurological samples and thus are not necessarily a sign of any type of disorder. Kellner and Sheffield (1973) indicated that approximately 90% of healthy individuals report that they experience some somatic symptoms during the course of a week. The most prevalent symptoms are headaches, fatigue, and muscle pain.

Ford (1983) suggested that somatization is a form of social and emotional communication. Sick role behavior can provide a source of control in interpersonal relationships. Although sick role behavior can be related to the onset of a neurological illness or accident, its etiology is wide ranging. For example, patients may be from families who minimize or discourage psychological distress but sanction somatic complaints. Evidence suggests that children who are implicitly reinforced for playing the sick role are more likely to adopt such a role later in life (Whitehead, Winget, Fedoravicius, Wooley, & Blackwell, 1981).

State Factors

Cimino (1994) identified a number of state factors—including poor attention, fatigue, poor motivation, secondary gain, and malingering—that can affect the validity and interpretability of intellectual or neuropsychological test results. Cimino contended that of all the participant-specific factors that are weighed when interpreting such data, state factors are some of the most important when determining the validity of test findings. Deficits in stamina or attentional process and other state factors can be caused by an overly lengthy evaluation process, inadequate rest breaks, or an inadequate amount of sleep prior to the examination. Anyone conducting cognitive testing should address these variables so that the patient may approach an optimal level of performance and test scores will be accurate.

Although the impact of state factors can render standard norms less useful and require greater qualification in the interpretation of test findings, the presence of such factors can actually increase the ecological validity of the assessment process. Indeed, evaluating the influence of fatigue or motivation might better approximate the functional abilities of the patient. Ideally, consideration of how the patient performs under optimal circumstances and how he or she performs when functioning is affected by a state factor, such as fatigue, provides clinicians with an appreciation of the patient's range of performance.

Psychological Consequences of Actual or Perceived Neurological Insult

The origins of symptoms that occur following neurological disturbance are complex and are both physiologic and psychological (Freed, 1997; Miller, 1991). Individuals who sustain neurological trauma also experience insult to ego functions, disrupting their perceptions of themselves as effectively adapting to the external world. The cognitive sequelae associated with moderate to severe neurological trauma produce tremendous adaptive deficits. Milder neurological injury or illness is accompanied by more optimistic recovery potential.

Psychological consequences of actual or perceived neurological insult fit into the psychosocial realm. The term *psychosocial* is used vaguely to encompass feelings, symptoms, and functional changes in patients, family members, and significant others. Understanding the nature and remediation of psychosocial problems subsequent to neurological insult or perceived neurological insult requires a refined definition of the term, at least as it relates to neuropsychological functioning and the process of differential diagnosis. One definition of psychosocial functioning is similar to Freud's definition of psychological health: the capacity to work and love. Indeed, these domains many times are the focus of complaints voiced by family members and significant others concerning postinjury changes in their loved ones. Psychosocial functioning as it relates to neuropsychologically impaired patients, then, means an individual's ability, and satisfaction with his or her ability, to perform social role activities within the community or society. This definition includes the capacity to negotiate the immediate environments of home or work, the ability to form and maintain meaningful relationships with others, and quality of life throughout these endeavors. McLean, Dikmen, Temkin, Wyler, and Gale (1984) asserted that blatant activities associated with physical functioning, such as mobility or self-care, often are less significant than subtle social performance factors related to work and familial relationships. Brooks (1992) identified three main psychosocial categories that are compromised following neurological insult: social and family life, occupational life, and recreational life.

Certain organic disorders have high potential for producing symptoms with emotional or psychiatric features. It is not uncommon to observe striking change in personality or symptoms characteristic of affective disturbance following cerebrovascular accidents. Similarly, epilepsy can produce dramatic changes in personality and behavior, including episodes of suspiciousness, religiosity, and rigidity. Binder and Rattok (1989) delineated a number of critical diagnostic concerns following head injury, including depression, anxiety disorders, substance abuse, somatoform disorders, vestibular problems, and dissimulation. Although they do not manifest a *DSM–IV* Axis I disorder, many patients who have traumatic neurological conditions (e.g., traumatic brain injury, stroke) commonly experience devastating personality changes following the event (Prigatano, 1987).

Following milder insults, patients may manifest cognitive and psychosocial changes that are more functional than organic in nature. For example, evidence of depression, anxiety, or personality change may exist, whereas evidence of severe memory, attentional, or visuospatial deficits does not. An absence of test results indicating such obvious cognitive deficits can cause a clinician to ignore the fact that subtle neuropathology-based cognitive decline is impairing the patient's capacity for adaptive psychic functioning. Indeed, patients with minimal cognitive deficits at times endure more disturbed ego functioning than patients who are too cognitively impaired to comprehend what is transpiring.

Individuals experiencing the psychological consequences of neurological disorders often begin their search for answers by consulting a psychotherapist or other mental health professional. Such a client's potentially misleading presentation can be intensified if these masquerading symptoms arise in the context of a troublesome life circumstance or other stressor.

Psychosocial variables are not only consequential to the differential diagnosis process, but they also are important in predicting outcomes of treatment because of their impact on interpersonal relationships, vocational success, and other factors. The ability to cope, for example, is one such aspect of psychosocial functioning. Malia, Powell, and Torode (1995) examined the relation between psychosocial functioning and coping style in a group of neurological patients of different etiologies. Patients and their relatives completed the Ways of Coping checklist, which revealed that neurological patients use four methods of coping: problem-focused strategies, emotion-focused strategies, avoidance, and wishful thinking. Poor levels of psychosocial functioning were correlated with the use of emotion-focused strategies, avoidance, or wishful thinking. The same conclusion also was reached for non-neurological medical populations. In another study of the relation between psychosocial functions and outcomes, Colantonio, Kasl, Ostfeld, and Berkman (1993) examined the influence of premorbid psychosocial factors on physical functioning and institutionalization following stroke in a group of old patients. Overall, the findings suggest that, in addition to the severity, nature, and comorbidity of the stroke, specific psychosocial factors have prognostic importance.

It is important to recognize that psychological symptoms can result from actual neurological insult, an exaggeration of the magnitude of neurological insult, or perceived rather than actual neurological insult. For example, someone who bumps his or her head may or may not incur neurological injury. If neurological injury is present, the person might experience either real psychological symptoms attributable to the injury or aggrandizement of real symptoms based on exaggerated magnitude of the injury. A third scenario is that the "bump on the head" does not result in neurological insult yet the individual perceives resultant psychological or cognitive symptoms. Exaggeration of symptoms or fixation on perceived symptoms, in turn, can produce real symptoms: an obsessive belief that one is experiencing memory problems can cause one to be distracted enough to have difficulty remembering things.

Changes in Personality and Related Psychological Characteristics

Bond (1975) maintained that psychosocial factors that were operational before neurological insult are more predictive of psychiatric illness than the brain damage itself. Indeed, premorbid personality seems to contribute to the manner in which changes in personality following neurological insult are expressed (Lishman, 1973), although Prigatano (1987) stipulated that the role of premorbid personality is more important in cases of mild head injury than in cases of severe head injury. The relation between premorbid psychological characteristics and postinjury or -illness function is less clear. Some individuals demonstrate an exaggeration of premorbid traits, such as aggressiveness or impulsivity; others exhibit diminished tendencies or the cessation of certain behaviors (Bond, 1984).

Stagle (1990) noted that patients who evidence emotional disturbance prior to a neurological event are more likely to develop postinjury psychiatric dysfunction. Similarly, patients who have a high degree of premorbid cognitive capacity fare better than others when faced with encroaching neurological decline, such as that from Alzheimer's disease. Thus, such individuals may be more capable of navigating the inevitable issues of despondency, helplessness, and loss that follow neurological insult. However, even patients with relatively little compromise of higher cognitive functions, such as abstract reasoning, are impaired in their adaptive functioning if their ego strength is incapable of tolerating anxiety, anger, and interpersonal contact.

Of course, issues of lateralization and location of injury are significant when evaluating patients who display changes in psychological or personality status. For example, Miller (1991) suggested that the right hemisphere is less involved in modifying inner needs in response to the demands and constraints of the outside world than the left hemisphere, which can alter external reality to meet inner needs and wishes. He asserted that the left-hemisphere language system organizes and gives conscious social meaning to and control over feelings and drives. Thus, when neurodevelopment is halted at a stage associated with nascent language development, a corresponding impoverishment of self-referential behavioral control exists. Miller (1987) also contended that an individual who undergoes a condition that increases frustration, stress, or social ambiguity (e.g., cerebrovascular disease) may revert to behavioral patterns more appropriate to an earlier age that include antagonistic–antisocial behaviors not sanctioned by today's mores. In addition, the etiologic nature of a disorder can affect the manner in which the clinician evaluates psychological change. Increased religious beliefs, suspiciousness, and changes in interpersonal interactional style are viewed differently in individuals with a history of temporal lobe epilepsy, for instance, than in individuals with no such history.

Independent of neurologically based changes following neurological insult or emergence of personality traits that had been inhibited prior to neurological insult, personality changes also may reflect an attempt to cope with disability. Lezak (1983) stated that personality changes often arise as a result of frustration, loss, and life difficulties. Depression, one of the most common emotional characteristics seen in brain-injured patients, may be a healthy sign that signals awareness of deficits (F. C. Goldstein & Levin, 1989). A family's reaction and response to disability also can entrench and maintain maladaptive responses by the patient. Brooks (1984) noted that the level of complaints voiced by relatives is associated with their own levels of neuroticism, as measured by the Eysenck Personality Inventory.

Affective Disorders

Because depression and other affective disorders may be the first symptoms reported for a variety of general medical conditions (Hall, Gardner, Stickney, LeCann, & Popkin, 1980), it is critical when evaluating a client who exhibits neuropsychological deficits to discern what degree of cognitive deficit is related to affective disturbance and what degree is related to the neurological condition alone. In general, data obtained from studies of cognitive abilities suggest that affective disorders disturb attention and concentration, ergo memory and visuospatial functions (Richards & Ruff, 1989). Lachner and Engel (1994) performed a meta-analysis on studies that attempted to differentiate depression and dementia using various tests of memory. Results showed a greater effect size (a statistical index that accounts for the level of meaningful difference) for memory tests that tapped delayed versus immediate retrieval, distraction prior to recall, and "high-capacity demand."

Somatization

Internalized anxiety and neuroanatomically related psychosomatic symptoms are associated with intact functioning of the right hemisphere (Smokler & Shevrin, 1979). When the left hemisphere is compromised, an imbalance in activity between the hemispheres causes an increase in expression of these right-hemisphere symptoms. People with neurological insult may exhibit hypochondriasis or somatization.

Hypochondriasis and *somatization* are terms used to describe two ways of expressing distress by means of physical or medical symptoms. Hypochondriasis includes disease conviction, disease fear, and bodily preoccupation. Freud's view of hypochondriasis is a withdrawal of interest from the external world to internal organs or functioning (Freud, 1914/1957). This provides some explanation for the decreased social integration and involvement that often accompanies neurological insult (Prigatano, 1987). Alternately, somatization can be viewed as a perceptual amplification of bodily sensations and symptoms and a means for interpersonal secondary rewards (Barsky & Klerman, 1983). This conceptualization provides a useful heuristic for examining the roles played by symptom exaggeration and lowered effort on formal neuropsychological testing for patients as they attempt to alert practitioners to their continuing distress.

Both *expectancy*, the heightened awareness and anticipation of further symptom development, and *attribution*, the tendency to misinterpret subsequent perceptions as evidence of dysfunction, contribute to the origin of somatic complaints after head injury (Mittenberg, DiGiulio, Perrin, & Bass, 1992; Putnam & Millis, 1994). Putnam and Millis (1994) explained how mildly head-injured clients attach meaning and significance to somatic or functional symptoms that accompany typical human experience—relatively common and benign symptoms, such as occasional gastrointestinal distress following a large meal or sweating, are reprocessed as resulting from the head injury. Likewise, individuals with head injuries sometimes blame their injuries for benign emotional, physiological, and memory symptoms they experience (Mittenberg et al., 1992). After a patient forms ideas about what symptoms to expect, selective attention leads to heightened awareness and potential misattribution of benign events or symptoms. This situation initiates a vicious cycle in which the preoccupation with perceived symptoms brings about real symptoms. Mittenberg et al. (1992) contended that this circular reinforcement pattern may account for symptom maintenance, even when neuropsychological findings are absent. Putnam and Millis further noted that when individuals have no clear explanation of what they are experiencing, psychosocial and contextual influences assume greater meaning in the attributive process.

Although this dynamic attributive process is often discussed within the context of mild traumatic brain injury, it is likely that any perceived neurological condition can trigger such a response. Thus, other diagnostic groups are not immune from this type of reaction to perceived central nervous system (CNS) dysfunction. This includes individuals who have incurred more than mild CNS damage; the process differs only in the level of actual CNS damage on which it is imposed.

Several external psychosocial factors contribute to the maintenance and chronicity of such an attributive process. Patients may be increasingly susceptible to the potentially inaccurate interpretations of providers or significant others regarding the origins of continued symptomology. Financial incentives may add to this pattern (Butcher & Harlow, 1987), but the opportunity to avoid social and vocational demands represents a more likely influence resulting in protective or avoidance behavior by the patient. This can ultimately lead to a cognitive schema in which the patient views him- or herself as defective and becomes resistant to further physical, psychological, or social pain or lowering of self-esteem. Such a mindset may lead to patients assuming the sick role and being unwilling to return to premorbid roles until they deem themselves "as good as new." This phenomenon may be inversely related to premorbid functional, social, and vocational competencies: An individual who received abundant reinforcement for his or her performance of social, familial, or vocational duties might be increasingly unwilling to lose face by prematurely returning to such roles.

As Mittenberg et al. (1992) suggested, this attributive process can reduce cognitive efficiency as patients become mired in nonproductive concerns about symptoms, declines from premorbid status, and current life difficulties. This response leaves the individual with few cognitive resources to undertake mental or functional endeavors. This situation also can diminish patients' performance on formal intellectual or neuropsychological assessment tasks; this is an issue that is rarely cited as a potential deterrent to optimal performance on such measures.

Conclusion

Although a neuropsychological referral provides insight into critical diagnostic and prognostic aspects of the client's cognitive, neurological, or developmental status, general psychologists are left to deal with enduring social, emotional, and functional consequences of brain dysfunction. After the neuropsychological assessment is concluded, the generalist must support and facilitate the client's reintegration into vital social, familial, and vocational roles. Along with supporting these functional returns, the clinician is also the critical resource for the client as he or she attempts to assimilate the perplexing psychological and social challenges that characterize long-term recovery from neurological disease or injury.

Additional Reading

Attention-Deficit Hyperactivity Disorder in Adults (Wender, 1995) integrates theoretical material with practical suggestions for assessing and treating individuals with the condition. Psychosocial aspects of mild head injury are comprehensively covered in "Psychosocial Factors in the Development and Maintenance of Chronic Somatic and Functional Symptoms Following Mild Traumatic Brain Injury" (Putnam & Millis, 1994) in *Advances in Medical Psychotherapy, 7,* 1–22.

5

Indicators of Neuropsychological Impairment

For general clinicians, awareness of various neurological or other medical conditions whose presentations resemble psychologically based disorders is vital for determining when more specialized neuropsychological referral is needed. Moreover, a refined knowledge of the specific presenting symptoms of neuropsychological involvement allows general clinicians to narrow the range of conditions a client might have. Clinicians can pass this information along to the neuropsychologist, thereby improving the accuracy of early screening or detection efforts. Neuropsychological disorders can be revealed by a client's clinical history, records, and behavior as well as by the results of both standard psychological tests and procedures specifically designed to detect cognitive involvement. Integration of these factors is critical for proper referral and case management. The case study at the end of this chapter provides an example of such integration.

Client Interview and Records

The client interview and records can evidence neuropsychological impairment and are critical components for generalists

attempting to determine if an individual is in need of neuropsychological services. The history-taking and interview
process is important for three primary reasons. First, the clinician may uncover either evidence of a definitive developmental or acquired neurological condition the patient has experienced or evidence of a risk factor that may have led to
neuropsychological symptoms. Second, the clinician can observe the client's behavior for signs or symptoms suggestive
of neurological dysfunction. Third, the clinician can establish
a level of expectation for neuropsychological evaluation by
informing the neuropsychologist of potential moderator variables, or factors that cause the examiner to interpret impaired test scores in a more benign way. Moderator variables
such as the client's age, level of education, level of premorbid
functioning, and vocational experiences affect the interpretation of formal neuropsychological test findings. Evidence
of decline from an overall level of premorbid intellectual
functioning is one of the best indications of cognitive compromise.

Interview Content

A general clinician conducting a neuropsychologically sensitive interview may organize the history taking and interview as he or she ordinarily does; however, some questions
may depart from the format of the typical general clinical
interview. The traditional content of the interview differs in
several ways when a neurological etiology is plausible. Appendix B contains a sample interview form.

Presenting problem. General clinicians may be less experienced in evoking a report of cognitive or neuropsychological symptoms than they are in eliciting clients' descriptions
of psychological symptoms. To obtain such information, the
clinician should inquire about the client's view of his or her
attentional, memory, language, sensory–perceptual, motor,
and higher order cognitive abilities. Have these abilities de-
clined recently? If so, what has been the rate or pattern of
the decline? The clinician should ask what functional significance these symptoms have had for the patient in his or her

activities of daily living, social interactions, and vocational performance. The clinician should keep in mind that mild memory difficulty related to reduced retrieval capacity could accompany symptoms of affective disturbance, or it might be evidence for the word-finding difficulties commonly seen in patients with Alzheimer's disease. If the client identifies presenting symptoms, the clinician should follow with questions concerning social, medical, psychological, financial, and living situation events that occurred around the time of symptom onset. Geriatric patients should be questioned carefully about such circumstances because of their increased exposure and vulnerability to certain aging-related events: They might view as minor or unrelated an event that can produce devastating effects on cognition. For example, drug interaction effects or cardiac surgery can produce a delirium.

Developmental and early medical history. Clinicians should begin questioning in this domain by asking about prenatal and neonatal history. Was the client's mother exposed to any recreational drugs, prescribed medications, environmental toxins, or infections during her pregnancy? It is important to inquire about the nature of the delivery and critical incidents surrounding the client's birth. For example, was delivery accomplished by means of Cesarean section? Were forceps required? Length of the gestation period, birth weight, and Apgar scores also should be noted.

Next, the interviewer should ask when and with what difficulties, if any, developmental milestones were reached. Postural, mobility, and language development should be assessed. At what age did the client first sit up independently? When did he or she begin to crawl? Walk? When was the first word spoken? The first sentence? These developmental markers often represent the earliest indications of serious neurological disease or trauma that will have consequences on significant emerging cognitive capacities.

Information concerning early medical events should be obtained. The interviewer should chronicle all serious illnesses, surgeries, and hospitalizations. It is also important to inquire about less dramatic physical events, such as periods of high fever, frequent ear infections, and seemingly insignificant falls and minor injuries. When these events occur at developmentally critical periods, they can lead to neuropsychological impairment that emerges gradually over the course of development. Encouraging the client to organize recall of significant events in 5-year increments may assist him or her in recalling and describing developmental events.

It is helpful at this point to try to obtain information about the client's level of premorbid functioning. Ideally, the clinician would like to compare future performance on evaluative measures with a standardized measure that was administered prior to any compromise of central nervous system status. However, such direct comparative baselines are rarely available, forcing the practitioner to compare elements such as the current Full Scale IQ with indirect estimates of premorbid functioning derived from historical, demographic, or other variables that have been shown to correlate highly with premorbid functioning. Obtaining and estimating premorbid levels of functioning are detailed in chapter 6.

Family medical and psychiatric history. Given the familial origin of certain developmental and neurological conditions, a detailed family medical and psychiatric history is warranted. Many neurologically significant disorders that might have affected family members (e.g., dementing illness) were poorly understood in the past and often are recalled as psychiatric conditions. For this reason, the interviewer should acquire behaviorally anchored descriptions of any disorder sustained by members of the client's family. Conditions with strong genetic origins, such as Huntington's disease or amyotrophic lateral sclerosis (Lou Gehrig's disease), should be considered during such questioning. Schizophrenia, bipolar illness, and other psychiatric conditions, as well as developmental disorders, also are significant given their neuropsychological ramifications, as described in chapter 4.

Educational and early psychosocial history. Understanding a client's level of, quality of, and interest in education provides a context in which to interpret subsequent neuropsychological test scores. The highest grade achieved begins to provide such a context, but it is as important to understand the client's level of motivation for the education process, reasons for not obtaining further education, best and worst classes or subjects, and special services (e.g., math tutoring, special education classes, speech/language therapy) received during the education process. Education records should be requested, because they provide information concerning the overall quality of the client's educational experience, areas of academic strength and weakness, and the nature of special services received, and they chronicle performance on various aptitude and ability tests. Many times such records form the basis for the estimate of premorbid functioning that is used as the comparative foundation when assessing the results of a neuropsychological evaluation.

Of equal importance is the client's psychosocial development during the school years. How did the client and the client's family view the education process? What was the nature of the client's social relationships during childhood? How much time did the client spend with friends? What was his or her level of activity in social activities or clubs? Answers to these questions can inform the clinician about changes the client has undergone relative to the current symptom picture.

Vocational history. Vocational history provides another barometer of premorbid functioning and interests and furnishes information that may dramatically affect prognostic conjecture, rehabilitation efforts, and plans for vocational re-entry. The clinician should ask questions about the client's responsibilities in previous vocational settings and about the quality of his or her relationships with superiors, coworkers, and subordinates. In many cases, problematic relationships with colleagues and poor social skills that occur premorbidly are predictive of failed vocational re-entry attempts.

Recent social history. Finally, the clinician should explore the client's recent psychosocial history, lifestyle (e.g., living situation, alcohol and tobacco use), and existing social support mechanisms. Psychosocial factors, such as quality of romantic relationships and family interactions, can affect psychological status and, in turn, compromise neuropsychological capacities or interfere with motivation to perform optimally on the neuropsychological evaluation. Consequently, it is impossible to acquire a complete understanding of the complex dynamics of a social system through tests alone. Instead, the clinician who is attempting to disentangle the multifaceted psychosocial world of the neurological patient must use an evaluation process that includes a thorough history, self-report of the patient, reports of significant others, and observation of the patient.

Client's Behavior During the Interview

Observation of a client during the interview and psychological testing process is critical to the issue of referral for neuropsychological services. Certain signs or behaviors can indicate the presence of neuropathologic processes requiring further workup. Such pathognomonic signs may be the first clues that additional neuropsychological evaluation is warranted. Many patients with neurological disorders may not display such signs; however, few individuals who do not have a neurological condition will display these abnormal signs. Thus, failure to find these signs, used in isolation or outside the context of historical variables, could lead to false negative conclusions (conclusions that a client does not have a disorder when, in reality, he or she does have the disorder). Besides these specific signs, the clinician should observe the client's casual behavior for general deficits that can be highly diagnostic.

Specific signs. The occurrence of certain signs or symptoms in a client's general appearance, sensory–perceptual functioning, motor abilities, and language capacity can reveal compromised neurological status.

The client's general appearance can suggest unilateral neuropathology in a number of ways. For example, individuals with right-hemisphere involvement occasionally exhibit a type of neglect in which they fail to dress adequately the left side of the body. Such an individual might fail to button a sleeve or collar on the left side (Kolb & Wishaw, 1996). Difficulty in chaining together the steps necessary to dress oneself properly might be evidence of a dressing apraxia (disturbance of some purposeful movement or sequence of movements; Filley, 1995). Another sign notable in a client's general appearance is ptosis (a drooping eyelid), which may signify that increased intracranial pressure is causing compression of certain nerves.

Although any form of sensory–perceptual decline might mean active neurological disease, some symptoms should raise immediate concerns. One such symptom is the visual field cut, in which a client experiences loss of vision in a portion of his or her field of vision. Such visual losses often are made evident by clients' continual attempts to relocate to the left or right reading materials or test stimuli placed directly in front of them. Until tested directly, this visual loss may not be obvious to the patient because the visual system accommodates for it relatively successfully (Kolb & Wishaw, 1996).

Abnormal movements of the body or a body part also can denote the onset of a neurological condition. Simply observing the manner in which a patient leaves the seat in the waiting room and enters the office can provide clues related to postural or gait disturbance. A stoop, unsteadiness while walking, a wide-based gait, and a tendency to drag one foot are examples of the types of impaired gait that signal neurological difficulties. To identify such problems, the clinician should first develop a sense of what constitutes normal gait: how the arms swing, how far apart the feet are, and how long a normal stride is (Taylor, 1990). Along with whole-body movement, the clinician should look for abnormal movements limited to specific regions or limbs. For example, Parkinson's disease often manifests in postural rigidity, a resting tremor of the hands, or characteristic "pill rolling" movements of the fingers. The eyes also may exhibit motor abnormalities, such as *nystagmus* (jerky movements), which often accompanies chronic alcohol abuse.

Frank difficulties in motor speech or word usage also provide information to the clinician. *Dysarthria*, a deficit in forming the sounds of speech because of weakness of the musculature surrounding the mouth, many times accompanies cerebrovascular accidents that affect other motor capacities. Dysarthria is often evident when a patient attempts to pronounce specific sounds, such as *th*. Other speech deficits are related to the use of language in general. A client might display mild difficulties in retrieving a specific word or phrase for a variety of reasons, but a frank inability to understand basic language in conversation or to communicate at a rudimentary level is usually a sign of neurological involvement (Taylor, 1990).

General signs. General aspects of a client's behavior that may be less blatant than the pathognomonic indicators just noted also should be monitored for diagnostic relevance. The client's competence in dealing with a scheduled appointment, for example, illustrates such capacities as attention, memory, geographic and spatial orientation, and overall level of functional independence. Noting whether the patient successfully and independently follows directions to find the examiner's office building, navigates within the building, and arrives on time provides data regarding the integrity of attention, memory, and basic spatial abilities. The manner and facility with which he or she interacts with office staff and other patients in the waiting area informs the clinician about a client's level of basic social or adaptive skills.

The clinical interview is a rich opportunity to observe attention, memory, and language capacity. Does the client efficiently track the line of questioning, or does he or she require reminders of the question asked? Does the client fail to recall what has been discussed earlier in the interview? Difficulty with these tasks can suggest deficits of attention or long-term memory. Similar responses to different lines of questioning may suggest elements of *perseveration*, a tendency toward redundancy that sometimes indicates frontal lobe pathology.

Requesting Additional Records and Information

General clinicians may receive data such as medical records prior to or at the first meeting with a client. After the interview the clinician may wish to pursue additional records (e.g., medical, academic, military, vocational) from institutions or agencies the client noted during the history taking and interview. It is possible, for example, that documentation of a developmental disorder diagnosed through the school system did not reach a hospital intake procedure. Information to help establish estimates of premorbid functioning might be found in military records of ability testing conducted when the client was inducted. Such material often does not make its way into medical and social history documents. Psychological records also are less commonly seen in the document transfer process. For reasons of confidentiality or greater sensitivity about how this information is processed, even extensive psychiatric treatment histories may be absent in the standard medical record. These additional sources can clarify the nature of previous medical, neurological, developmental, or psychological conditions related to the client's current symptom picture.

The clinician may wish to request additional information directly from a client's family. Even after the family has been interviewed, it may be useful to get more information about a specific aspect of the client's current behavior or academic or medical history. Specific questionnaires about the client's health or behavior completed by the family can provide information about an event or illness with neuropsychological implications. Existing standard neuropsychological history questionnaires are useful in gathering this type of information. The Neuropsychological History Questionnaire (Wolfson, 1985) and the Neuropsychological Status Examination (Psychological Assessment Resources, 1983) efficiently cover these areas and can be completed by the client's family. The clinician also might devise a standard form customized to his or her specific practice characteristics.

Traditional Psychological Testing

Traditional psychological testing also can provide clues about neuropsychological impairment. Because of the manifold ways psychological testing can be affected by non-neurological factors, research suggests that use of any objective or projective measure expressly to diagnose the presence or absence of brain dysfunction is inappropriate and ineffective (Chelune, Ferguson, & Moehle, 1986). However, some commonly administered instruments can provide indications of cognitive problems that, when integrated with other clinical observations and evidence from the case history, can be useful in referring patients for comprehensive neuropsychological evaluation.

Minnesota Multiphasic Personality Inventory and Minnesota Multiphasic Personality Inventory–2

Some investigators have attempted to show relations between neuropathology and personality test profile types. Many such ad hoc "organic" diagnostic scales for the Minnesota Multiphasic Personality Inventory (MMPI), however, have been found to hold little utility in differentiating various neurological populations from psychiatric samples (Golden, Sweet, & Osmon, 1979; Watson, 1971). Contradictions within the literature have caused some neuropsychologists to assert that the MMPI was not constructed for neuropsychological assessment and may be inherently inappropriate for this purpose (Lezak, 1995).

Using the MMPI to diagnose or lateralize brain dysfunction clearly is not appropriate, yet some associated profile trends are more frequently found in the protocols generated by neuropsychological populations. For example, Kelland, Bennett, Mercer, Caroselli, and Del Dotto (1995) found elevations on Clinical Scales 1 and 3 and elevation on the Health Concerns content scale. Artzy (1995) found similar elevations on Scales 1 and 3, along with elevations on 2, 7, and 8, in both male and female patients referred for evaluation of possible head injury. Consequently, general clinicians should not view MMPI results as completely nonindicative of potential neurological involvement.

The most important recommendation for clinicians who are trying to make sense of these elevations is to develop an awareness of the manner in which a neurological patient might respond to specific types of items. For example, a traumatically brain injured patient might achieve elevation on Scale 8 by endorsing items reflective of his or her altered neurological status (e.g., diminished sensation, paralysis, forgetfulness) rather than indicating the presence of bizarre sensory experiences or delusional processes. Detailed inspection of critical items and understanding of how content can have unique meaning for individuals with organic dysfunction enables the clinician to better understand and utilize Minnesota Multiphasic Personality Inventory–2 (MMPI–2) findings with neurological patients.

The Personality Assessment Inventory (Morey, 1991) is an alternative objective instrument that has promise for application in neuropsychological populations (Sweet & Westergaard, 1997). This measure's assistive features include a briefer length and relatively lower required reading level (fourth grade).

Rorschach Test

The Rorschach test is a commonly administered projective instrument that taps many process aspects of personality structure. Throughout the years, researchers have tried to identify specific markers for "organicity," or neuropathologic conditions, that would permit identification of cerebrally impaired individuals. Rorschach (1951) observed that cerebrally impaired individuals display illogical combinatory responses; display inconsistent succession of form level and area used; tend to give animal, human detail, and original responses; and produce only 30%–40% good form responses. Formal systems to screen for organicity were contributed by Oberholzer (1931) and Piotrowski (1937). Some authors have even found statistically meaningful differences among neuropsychological populations with different sites of lesion.

In spite of such findings, use of only the Rorschach as a screening measure for organicity is discouraged; however, the test can provide secondary information concerning neuropsychological status that is useful when coupled with other sources of clinical information. Lezak (1995) noted that responses to the test can be examined as an index of the patient's perceptual abilities, ability to process and integrate multiple stimuli, certainty of his or her own perceptions, and reaction time. Current studies with the Rorschach focus on differences between neurologically intact individuals and specific neuropathologic populations. For example, Perry, Potterat, Auslander, and Kaplan (1996) conducted a study in which they used a new scale that differentiated individuals with Alzheimer's disease from healthy older individuals. In addition, Exner, Colligan, Boll, and Stircher (1996) found that traumatically brain injured people, when compared with healthy individuals, demonstrate impoverishment of available resources, inconsistency in coping and decision making, simplistic ways of attending to details, unwillingness or inability in dealing with feelings and emotional stimulation, and lack of common social skills for promoting and maintaining meaningful relationships. Pediatric applications include an investigation by Bartell and Solanto (1995) that suggests that children diagnosed with attention-deficit/hyperactivity disorder display fewer human movement responses, poorer form quality, and a lower ratio of human movement and whole-figure responses.

Thematic Apperception Test

The Thematic Apperception Test (Murray, 1943/1971) is also inappropriate as a neuropsychological screening or diagnostic measure yet helpful in providing information relevant to neuropsychological difficulties (Lezak, 1995). Individuals with brain damage tend to display word-finding deficits, concrete descriptions of the picture or fewer ideas in their response, response time delays relative to control respondents, sequencing difficulties in organizing the story, an overall inability to interpret the picture holistically, a paucity of ideas, and perseveration in content or description. The content of the Thematic Apperception Test also may reflect personal reaction to the injury or deficit (Spreen & Strauss, 1998).

Wechsler Adult Intelligence Scale–III/Wechsler Intelligence Scale for Children–III

The Wechsler scales can generate much diagnostic information related to potential neuropsychological impairment (Wechsler, 1997a). In fact, it was initially hoped that the Wechsler scales would detect brain damage (Wechsler, 1958). A particular concept thought to have diagnostic potential was comparison of "hold" versus "no-hold" subtests of the Wechsler Adult Intelligence Scale (WAIS, Wechsler, 1997a). Hold subtests (e.g., Vocabulary) were viewed as resistant to the effects of brain damage, and no-hold subtests (e.g., Block Design) were seen as sensitive to the effects of brain damage. It was thought that large discrepancies between the hold and no-hold tests reflect greater possibility of brain damage. The notion that the Wechsler scales can detect brain damage has not been supported universally, and use of the WAIS as a single diagnostic indicator of brain damage has not been successful, largely because of the following reasons, suggested by Vogt and Heaton (1977):

- Brain damage has no single pattern, so highly variable test responses are to be expected.
- The hold–no-hold distinction does not account for other significant factors, such as age when brain damage occurred, environmental variables, education, location of the lesion, and whether a lesion is recent or long standing.
- Many important abilities related to brain damage are not measured by the WAIS–R or the Wechsler Intelligence Scale for Children–III (WISC–III; Wechsler, 1991).

Although several additions to the WAIS–III have improved its sensitivity to brain dysfunction relative to its predecessor, many of Vogt and Heaton's (1977) concerns are still valid. Obviously, isolated use of the WAIS–III as an indictor of brain damage is not warranted, but its use as part of a general clinician's inventory in deciding when to refer for neuropsychological evaluation is supported.

The best overall indicator of neuropsychological dysfunction emerging from the WAIS–III is a perceived significant decline from a premorbid level of functioning. As the discrepancy between the premorbid estimate and the current Full Scale IQ generated by the WAIS–III expands (generally beyond one standard deviation), it is increasingly likely that the client has experienced a decline in cognitive status from premorbid levels. Another potential marker of neurological compromise in WAIS–III results is the difference between Verbal (VIQ) and Performance (PIQ) subscale scores. This difference alone cannot be used as an immutable sign of organicity; however, a statistically significant and clinically meaningful discrepancy that is unexpected when viewed in light of other clinical and historical case material should prompt concern on the part of the clinician. For example, obtaining a 25-point split in favor of the Performance IQ in a college law professor (e.g., VIQ = 85, PIQ = 110) should raise suspicions and lead to comprehensive neuropsychological evaluation. Although a difference of 12 points is statistically significant, Kaufman and Lichtenberger (1999) suggested that a difference of 17 points is required for a discrepancy to be considered abnormal.

Evidence of more generalized neuropathologic involvement may arise from inspection of WAIS–III subtests that are most sensitive to diffuse brain damage. Although focal injuries selectively can impair virtually any group of subtests, more diffuse neurological injuries or illnesses often take their greatest toll on attention or concentration, some aspect of memory, and general speed of cognitive processing.

The Digit Symbol Coding subtest is one of the least helpful subtests in localizing potential lesion sites but is perhaps the most sensitive indicator of diffuse neuropathology (Lezak, 1995). Reasons for this sensitivity include the significant time demands inherent in the test and the multidomain cognitive requirements of the task (e.g., visual scanning, attention, working memory, and the capacity to write or draw). These cognitive components involve relatively large cognitive networks subserved by equally large areas of cortical and subcortical structures. Thus, damage in a variety of brain regions can produce compromise of one or more of the cognitive domains required for optimal performance on the Digit Symbol Coding subtest.

The frequent symptoms of decreased attention, concentration, or processing speed also may be revealed through the Digit Span, Letter–Number Sequencing, and Arithmetic subtests of the WAIS–III. Comparing these time- or attention-dependent subtests with overlearned abilities is helpful following some types of diffuse neurological insult.

Finally, patients who have sustained diffuse neurological involvement often manifest deficits in abstract reasoning, or "taking the abstract attitude," in K. Goldstein's (1952) vernacular. This lack of cognitive flexibility can produce a type of fixedness, or concrete thinking, that emerges on specific WAIS–III subtests. Inspection of both level of performance and the qualitative nature of responses on subtests such as Similarities, Comprehension, and Matrices is diagnostically meaningful when interpreted within the context of the client's educational, social, vocational, and medical history.

In summary, although the Wechsler scales have not been supported as definitive stand-alone indicators of brain dysfunction, developing an awareness of which patterns make neuropsychological sense in the context of other client information can be valuable for general clinicians. This awareness allows practitioners to make better informed decisions concerning consultation, referral for comprehensive neuropsychological examination, and treatment.

Bender–Gestalt

Although some researchers have cautioned against using the Bender–Gestalt as a sole screening device for brain damage (Bigler & Ehrfurth, 1980; Franzen & Berg, 1998), it often is included as part of a general assessment of psychological status and has shown sensitivity to certain forms of brain damage. Specifically, impaired performance is associated with parietal lesions (Crawford, Parker, & McKinlay, 1992). A clinician who routinely uses the Bender as part of a standard psychological assessment battery may derive value from a knowledge of the difficulties that can accompany neurological dysfunction. Several qualitative features of the Bender–Gestalt occur more frequently with neurologically impaired groups. For example, patients with right-hemisphere damage are more susceptible to errors of rotation, where reproduction of test stimuli is oriented incorrectly in relation to the model (Billingslea, 1963). In general, Bender error scores have shown success in predicting functional status or decline in specific neurological illness as well (Acker & Davis, 1989; Wolber & Lira, 1981).

The Canter Background Interference Procedure is an adjunctive procedure that can increase the sensitivity of the Bender–Gestalt in revealing difficulties with brain-damaged patients (Canter, 1976). With this method, the patient is initially given the standard administration of the Bender and then asked to reproduce the designs on sheets of paper covered with wavy black lines. Scoring and interpretation of this method involves a comparison of the two administrations of the test. Correct classification rates across studies have resulted in a median classification rate of 84% when incorporating the Canter procedure (Heaton, Baade, & Johnson, 1978).

Tests of Academic Achievement

Tests of achievement usually are not viewed as central to the task of evaluating neuropsychological status and referral for additional evaluative services, but they may have utility in specific circumstances. Understanding the neuropsychological application of academic achievement measures is helpful to general clinicians who use these tests for routine types of evaluations (e.g., psychoeducational).

First, achievement tests provide critical baseline data that are relevant to estimates of premorbid functioning. The Wide Range Achievement Test–Third Edition is an achievement measure that is used, along with other demographic variables, in a formula to estimate premorbid intellectual functioning. Second, achievement tests can be sensitive to certain forms of neuropsychological problems related to verbal and symbolic interpretation and manipulation. For example, some patients with parietal lobe injuries manifest deficits in spelling skills, even when attempting relatively simple words (Golden, 1979). Application of the Woodcock–Johnson Psycho-Educational Battery–Revised (Woodcock & Johnson, 1989) to neuropsychological assessment has been closely examined (Woodcock, 1998). Woodcock (1998) noted that, along with the expected purpose of providing information concerning academic achievement, the battery provides information relevant to the neuropsychological domains of attention, visual perception/processing, auditory perception/processing, memory and learning, language, and reasoning and problem solving. Third, measures of academic achievement provide information related to neuropsychological deficits of a developmental nature. Tests such as the Woodcock–Johnson or the Wechsler Individual Achievement Test (Psychological Corporation, 1992) provide indispensable information concerning the presence of formal learning disabilities (e.g., reading, written expression).

Specific Procedures for Detecting Cognitive Involvement

Detecting neuropsychological impairment also may involve using procedures directly developed for the task of determining cognitive involvement. *Neuropsychological screening* refers to the application of test findings in designating individuals who require further neuropsychological evaluation to determine if they manifest a particular disorder. The screening device comprises a small number of tests and procedures that can be applied routinely, efficiently, and economically. An effective screening device yields a very low frequency (near zero) of false negative and false positive conclusions (Rourke, Bakker, Fisk, & Strang, 1983).

Over the years, many investigators have attempted to identify a single test as *the* screening device that differentiates patients with brain damage from those without brain damage. In virtually all instances, such attempts have failed. The many reasons for single tests failing to effectively differentiate the two populations include the following:

- □ No single measure can tap all areas of brain functioning. For example, the Bender–Gestalt is ill suited to detect subtle aspects of language impairment, and the Speech Perception Test of the Halstead–Reitan Battery (Macciocchi & Barth, 1996) does not address the visuospatial difficulties that often follow right-hemisphere involvement.
- □ It can be difficult to distinguish which aspects of task failure are related to general capacity and the client's premorbid level of functioning and which are related instead to the acquired deficits of brain dysfunction.
- □ Because some individual screening tests target only specific behaviors, using just one such test less accurately gauges brain damage than using a battery of tests (Sox, Blatt, Higgins, & Morton, 1988).

Specifying what conditions a neuropsychological evaluation is intended to screen for significantly narrows the focus of the examination and subsequently improves its diagnostic utility. In many cases, specifying the intention of the evaluation clarifies the nature of the diagnostic question and suggests that a more comprehensive assessment is needed.

It is important to realize that in some cases investigation other than neuropsychological screening is mandated. If evidence suggests an active neurological condition that has not been treated medically, immediate referral to a physician clearly is more appropriate than neuropsychological screening or comprehensive neuropsychological evaluation. When it is clear that a developmental or neuropsychological condition (e.g., learning disability, traumatic brain injury) exists, comprehensive neuropsychological assessment rather than neuropsychological screening is warranted, as developmental and neuropsychological conditions are unlikely to lend themselves to brief screening technology. No current screening tests perform at a level that would result in no false negatives or false positives. A third scenario arises when there is a need to assess a known but not currently medically significant disorder. In this case, a neuropsychological screening is not necessary to determine a known fact. Even if the question is related to the consequence rather than the existence of the disorder, the question remains: "Are screening tests adequate to determine whether a comprehensive evaluation is needed?" and the answer is no.

Global Measures of Neuropsychological Status

Because of the problems associated with screening for neuropsychological disorders, few available instruments have unchallenged diagnostic power in detecting a given neurobehavioral syndrome. However, when the diagnostic alternatives can be narrowed to some extent, and the clinician carefully integrates alerting signs from other sources, such as the interview, routine psychological test findings, and behavioral observations, with a sound measure of overall neuropsychological status, incremental validity is improved. Three such global cognitive status scales can provide the general clinician with important information and are superior to single-test screening measures for a number of reasons. For example, these tests include several scales, or subtests, that evaluate various cognitive domains, thereby increasing each instrument's sensitivity to multiple conditions that affect neurobehavioral status. Guidelines used to select and evaluate measures for potential use as cognitive screens are listed in Table 5.1.

Neurobehavioral Cognitive Status Examination. This general battery assesses independent areas of cognition in an attempt to identify individuals with neuropsychological impairment (Schwamm, VanDyke, Kiernan, Merrin, & Mueller, 1987). Rather than generating a total or summative score, as is the case with most screening measures, the Neurobehavioral Cognitive Status Examination (NCSE) provides separate domain scores in 10 cognitive areas, as shown in Figure 5.1.

Each area contains a number of items that range in difficulty level and includes one screening item. If a client passes the screening item, no additional items within that area are

Table 5.1

Guidelines for Evaluating Cognitively Sensitive Measures

Area of concern	Evaluation questions
Normative relevance	Are the test norms appropriate to the client being evaluated? Is the size of the normative sample adequate?
Psychometric issues	Is the measure sufficiently sensitive and specific to the condition being assessed? Is the measure reliable internally and across time? Is the measure valid for the purpose for which it is being used?
Pragmatic issues	Is the instrument appropriate for the client (e.g., reading level, educational background)? Is the measure cost effective in terms of financial expense, time required for administration, and the demands placed on the client in completing it? Is the measure appropriate for assessing changes in neuropsychological status over time?

presented, and performance within that domain is assumed to be intact. If the client fails the screening item, he or she is given less difficult items within that domain so that an accurate estimate of performance level can be established. The NCSE's screening component increases the efficiency of the measure, allowing it to be routinely administered and scored within 20–30 min. Administration of only the screening items has been associated with an increased false negative rate. Because the format of the NCSE allows evaluation of multiple cognitive domains, the test is suitable for documenting the cognitive decline that accompanies disease progression (Margolin, 1992). Lezak (1995) cautioned that the Attention and Speech and Language scales of the NCSE should be supplemented with more difficult items in order to record the relatively subtle but troublesome problems that can occur in those areas.

Dementia Rating Scale. The Dementia Rating Scale (DRS; Mattis, 1988) was devised as an alternative to standardized

COGNISTAT
(THE NEUROBEHAVIORAL COGNITIVE STATUS EXAMINATION)

NAME: _____   OCCUPATION: _____

AGE: _____ DATE OF BIRTH: _____   DATE LAST WORKED: _____

HANDEDNESS (circle):   Left   Right   DATE OF INJURY (if any): _____

NATIVE LANGUAGE: _____   EXAM LOCATION: _____

TOTAL YEARS EDUCATION: _____   DATE: _____ TIME: _____

COGNITIVE STATUS PROFILE

	LOC	ORI	ATT	LANGUAGE			CONST	MEM	CALC	REASONING	
				COMP	REP	NAM				SIM	JUD
							--6--			--8--	--6--
†AVG. RANGE	ALERT	--12--	--(S)8--	--(S)6--	--(S)--	--(S)--	--(S)5--	--12--	--(S)4--	--(S)6--	--(S)5--
					--12--	--8--					
		--10--	--6--	--5--	--11--	--7--	--4--	--10--	--3--	--5--	--4--
MILD	--IMP--	--8--	--5--	--4--	--9--	--5--	--3--	--8--	--2--	--4--	--3--
MODERATE		--6--	--3--	--3--	--7--	--3--	--2--	--6--	--1--	--3--	--2--
SEVERE		--4--	--1--	--2--	--5--	--2--	--0--	--4--	--0--	--2--	--1--
Write in lower scores											

ABBREVIATIONS

ATT	-	Attention	JUD	-	Judgment	ORI	-	Orientation
CALC	-	Calculations	LOC	-	Level of	REP	-	Repetition
COMP	-	Comprehension			Consciousness	S	-	Screen
CONST	-	Constructions	MEM	-	Memory	SIM	-	Similarities
IMP	-	Impaired	NAM	-	Naming			

*The validity of this examination depends on administration in strict accordance with the Cognistat Manual.

† For patients over the age of 65 the average range extends to the "mild impairment" level for Constructions, Memory and Similarities.

Note: Not all brain lesions produce cognitive deficits that will be detected by Cognistat. Normal scores, therefore, cannot be taken as evidence that brain pathology does *not* exist. Similarly, scores falling in the mild, moderate, or severe range of impairment do not *necessarily* reflect brain dysfunction (see section of the Cognistat Manual entitled "Cautions in Interpretations").

© Copyright 1983, 1988, 1995. No portion of this Test Booklet may be copied, duplicated, or otherwise reproduced without the prior written consent of the copyright owner.

**The Northern California
Neurobehavioral Group, Inc.
P.O. Box 460
Fairfax, CA 94978
Telephone: (800) 922-5840**

Revised 5/

Figure 5.1.   Profile summary of the Cognistat (Neurobehavioral Cognitive Status Examination).

cognitive or intellectual tests (e.g., the WAIS–III). Demented or profoundly impaired geriatric patients produce few valid responses on comprehensive or difficult measures, so the DRS was designed as a method for quantifying the neuropsychological status of such individuals (Mattis, 1988). DRS items are organized hierarchically so that success on an item within a given subscale allows the examiner to discontinue that subscale and assume adequate performance on subsequent items. This hierarchical format allows the DRS to be efficiently administered in 15–45 min to healthy elderly people as well as to individuals with cognitive difficulties. In constructing the DRS, Mattis (1988) arranged items according to face validity into five subscales, or domains: Attention, Memory, Construction, Initiation and Perseveration, and Conceptualization. Along with scores for each of the five subscales the DRS produces a total score with a maximum of 144 raw points. The DRS has adequate convergent and predictive validity (Spreen & Strauss, 1998). The overall score on the DRS was initially intended to differentiate between demented and nondemented elderly individuals, but it also may distinguish among dementias of specific etiologies, such as Alzheimer's disease or Parkinson's disease (Paolo, Troster, Glatt, Hubble, & Koller, 1994).

Barrow Neurological Institute Screen. The Barrow Neurological Institute Screen (BNIS) is a multidomain instrument that may have advantages over most cognitive screening measures because of the assessment needs it proposes to evaluate. The test's purposes are to

- ☐ determine when a client is capable of undergoing neuropsychological testing,
- ☐ provide qualitative information regarding cognitive functioning,
- ☐ screen the range of higher cerebral functions, and
- ☐ examine a patient's awareness of his or her current cognitive and emotional status.

The BNIS contains 38 scorable items and can be administered to most patients in 20–30 min. Items making up the

BNIS contribute to one of the following seven subscales: Speech and Language Functions, Orientation, Attention/Concentration, Visuospatial and Visual Problem Solving, Memory, Affect, and Awareness (self-awareness) Versus Performance. Test–retest coefficients for the seven subtests range from .31 to .93. The overall test–retest reliability of the BNIS is estimated at .93–.97. The diagnostic validity of the BNIS is adequate and suggests an average difference of 10 points when control respondents and patients are compared (Prigatano, Amin, & Rosenstein, 1993). Although sensitivity to brain dysfunction—that is, correctly classifying neurological patients as having a particular disorder—is strong (97%), the measure has low specificity—the ability to correctly classify individuals as not having a particular disorder—when a cutoff score of 47 is used (Prigatano et al., 1993). Although both sensitivity and specificity are critical, it may be imperative for general clinicians that no individual requiring neuropsychological evaluation and services be missed. Thus, erring on the side of caution by using an instrument that possesses higher sensitivity than specificity might be an appropriate compromise.

Screening Measures for Specific Cognitive Domains

As discussed, the detection capacity of cognitive measures is greatly enhanced by narrowing the etiologic and diagnostic contexts. Choosing tests that are most appropriate for the individual (e.g., DRS for geriatric patients) and the diagnostic population in which one suspects the individual falls (e.g., brain injury, stroke) increases the diagnostic power of composite screening scales. Similarly, detailed evaluation of specific symptom patterns also improves diagnostic detection and the subsequent referral for comprehensive neuropsychological assessment. Tests designed to assess the integrity of a specific aspect of cognitive functioning assist the referring clinician. First, many measures of focal cognitive domains possess some more difficult items that more sensitively detect subtle neuropsychological decline. Using these instruments in conjunction with general neuropsychological tests, behavioral observations, and a thorough understanding of the client's history adds to the predictive validity of the evaluation process. A second reason for the inclusion of domain-specific tasks relates to the focal nature of some neuropathologic conditions. In cases of mild closed head injury, general cognitive screening tests will indicate that basic mental status has been spared, whereas tests of executive-control functioning might show the specific cognitive deficits that follow damage to the parts of the frontal lobes most vulnerable to head trauma. Finally, use of specific tests may allow the referring clinician to provide the neuropsychologist with more complete or useful information about presenting cognitive symptoms.

Selecting Tests

To assist the clinician in using norms that are appropriate for the client being evaluated, numerous normative studies for each of several common neuropsychological measures are now available. Table 5.2 contains a list of suggested tests that meet most of these criteria and serve as useful domain-specific measures for clinicians wishing to tap more focal cognitive symptoms.

Case Study

Mr. A, age 29, was referred for a general psychological exam at the request of his employer. Mr. A was said to have become increasingly socially immature, impulsive, and labile in the workplace. These changes had manifested in reduced productivity and competence. The requested evaluation was intended to provide an explanation of how these "psychological" issues might be treated to assist Mr. A in regaining his previous level of occupational capacity.

When interviewed by the psychologist, Mr. A displayed no obvious language difficulties as he described his difficulties at work. His speech was marked by mild problems articu-

Table 5.2

Neuropsychological Tests

Domain of interest	Test	Approximate time to administer test
Attention and concentration	Trail Making Test	5–10 min
	Brief Test of Attention	5 min
Memory	Rey Auditory Verbal Learning Test	25–30 min
Language	Boston Naming Test	5–10 min
	Verbal Fluency	5 min
Motor	Finger Tapping Test	5–10 min
	Grooved Pegboard	5 min
Visuoperceptual/ visuospatial	Hooper Visual Organization Test	5 min
	Visual Form Discrimination	5 min
Executive-control functions and problem-solving	Wisconsin Card Sorting Test	20–30 min
	Stroop Test	5–10 min

lating certain sounds (e.g., *th*). In addition, his posture during the interview appeared to be somewhat rigid. Finally, although he performed within the average (scaled score = 10) on the Block Design subtest of the WAIS–III, he had difficulty with physically placing the blocks. This difficulty appeared to be directly related to a slight tremor, which was observed during his performance on this and other motor tasks.

Formal testing revealed a significant impairment on the Picture Arrangement and Comprehension subtests of the WAIS–III and a relative weakness on subtests demanding intact attention and concentration (i.e., Letter–Number Sequencing, Digit Span, Arithmetic).

On the MMPI–2 Mr. A displayed a moderate elevation on Scale 8 (schizophrenia; T score = 70). However, closer inspection of the items contributing to Scale 8 revealed that the items Mr. A had endorsed were related more to declines in cognitive abilities and complaints of neurological changes than to bizarre thought content or delusional processes.

On the basis of observation of behavior and formal test findings, Mr. A was referred to a neurologist, who diagnosed Mr. A as having Wilson's disease (a genetic condition resulting in abnormal copper metabolism). Subsequent treatment aimed at reducing intake of copper and increasing efficiency of copper elimination in Mr. A's body was helpful in reversing much of his behavioral and neurological symptomology.

Conclusion

Perhaps the most important knowledge for general clinicians to possess is an understanding of the manner in which various neurological and other medical conditions resemble or initially masquerade as psychological in origin. The ability to differentiate between psychological disturbance and neurological conditions with psychological sequelae is critical in determining when more specialized neuropsychological referral is warranted. This knowledge of the specific presenting symptoms of neuropsychological involvement allows general clinicians to better identify the focus of subsequent neuropsychological referral. In addition, this understanding alleviates redundancy when the client is interviewed by the neuropsychologist.

Additional Reading

A significant portion of the book *Screening for Brain Impairment: A Manual for Mental Health Practice* (2nd ed., Berg, Franzen, & Wedding, 1994) is devoted to a comprehensive review of tests useful to general clinicians. Related to the issue of using more relevant norms that are appropriate for the client being evaluated, *Handbook of Normative Data for Neuropsychological Assessment* (Mitrushina, Boone, & D'Elia, 1999) is useful. This book summarizes numerous normative studies for each of several common neuropsychological measures. A well-structured format for conducting a neuropsychologically oriented review of records can be found in *Clinical Neuropsychology: A Pocket Handbook for Assessment* (Snyder & Nussbaum, 1998).

III

Making Referrals

6

The Neuropsychological Referral Process

The ultimate goals of referring clients for neuropsychological assessment are to uniquely contribute to the understanding of an individual client and to optimize care of that client. These goals are most effectively met only when general clinicians appreciate how best to refer clients to neuropsychology professionals and to use feedback from the neuropsychologist. Also important is a knowledge of what happens between referral and the completed report: the neuropsychological assessment process. Knowing how to perform a neurologically sensitive evaluation, as discussed in chapter 5, is a good basis for understanding neuropsychological assessment, as the two evaluation processes share characteristics.

Referring Clients to Neuropsychology Professionals

Because comprehensive neuropsychological evaluations differentiate among brain-damaged, psychiatric, and normal populations, it would seem justifiable to administer comprehensive neuropsychological assessments to all patients suspected of having neurological disorders (Berg, Franzen, & Wedding, 1994). However, a general clinician might be unable to offer such services to all appropriate clients for a number of reasons. Given the relatively intensive training guidelines approved by Division 40 of the American Psychological Association, many general clinicians do not have the requisite training to conduct comprehensive neuropsychological examinations or the desire to obtain such training. Second, the neuropsychological evaluation process is time consuming and may not be accommodated by the schedule of a busy general clinician who sees five to seven patients per day. Finally, the cost of neuropsychological testing apparatuses may be prohibitive for a clinician for whom neuropsychological assessment is only a small segment of the overall practice. For these reasons, general clinicians should have a solid understanding of when a referral for more specialized services is needed.

Referring for a neuropsychological evaluation or neuropsychological consultation is often necessary or helpful in making diagnostic, treatment, and case management decisions. Various neurodiagnostic tools have eliminated the need for some neuropsychological assessment related to lesion localization; however, some diagnostic decision making continues to be aided by comprehensive neuropsychological assessment. In addition, decisions regarding how to treat a patient, or whether existing treatment is effective, can be improved by the neuropsychological evaluation. Finally, documenting the trajectory or velocity of cognitive change and the functional domains affected is helpful to a general clinician who must marshal resources, prepare caregivers, and make general case management decisions.

The context or reason for a neuropsychological referral is perhaps the most important determinant of the questions that will be posed to the neuropsychologist. If the referral is intended to answer questions related to vocational capacity, the referring clinician should ask the most specific questions possible, because the evaluation process and resulting neuropsychological report will more validly and directly address vocational concerns that are focally presented. Listed in Exhibit 6.1 are questions that may be helpful in clarifying a client's vocational abilities as they relate to neuropsychological functioning. When the neuropsychological evaluation is intended to address concerns related to the client's potential to benefit from rehabilitative or psychotherapeutic efforts, the particular referral questions will be quite different. In this context, inquiring about the client's potential strengths and weaknesses, learning capacity, and motivation for additional services are given greater credence. General clinicians can use Appendix C, an example of a neuropsychological referral

---

Exhibit 6.1

Questions for Clarifying Vocational Abilities

---

1. What level of supervision (guidance and structure) is required for this individual to function competently?
2. What individual and/or family psychodynamics will exacerbate neuropsychological deficits to further impair employment?
3. What is this individual's level of insight into his or her neuropsychological deficits and willingness to compensate for such deficits on the job?
4. What are this individual's stamina and endurance levels as these relate to his or her ability to engage in full-time employment?
5. How is this individual likely to respond to on-the-job stresses, such as time pressure, and off-the-job stresses, such as domestic life?
6. What is this individual's level of motivation for work, and what disincentives exist?
7. Given adequate motivation for employment, does this individual possess the cognitive ability to initiate and remain focused on job tasks?
8. How consistently well does this individual perform simple tasks? (Will this person's error rate due to distractions, confusion, etc., be too great to perform competently?)
9. What difficulties, if any, may this individual encounter in social and interpersonal interactions on the job?
10. Is this individual able to identify his or her own errors?
11. If an error is made, and it is identified or pointed out to this individual, is he or she able to correct the error?

worksheet, as an aid to gathering and organizing referral information.

The Assessment Process

Neuropsychological assessment occurs for a number of reasons: to assist with diagnosis, to aid in treatment planning or case management, to help relatives or caregivers prepare for a client's future needs, to evaluate the effectiveness of a medication trial or other intervention, to clarify various legal issues, or to track the ongoing course of an identified disorder or condition. The examination typically initially is dictated by the specific referral question posed, diagnostic issues inherent in the case, and the nature and severity of the patient's symptoms or neurological history.

Clarifying the Referral Question

To begin, a neuropsychologist must evaluate the appropriateness of the referral question. A referral might be overly vague, for example, requesting that the neuropsychologist assess a patient's "functional status." Although the question of functional capacity is appropriate for neuropsychological investigation, greater specificity is needed for the question to be of practical value. Focused questions, such as "Is the patient capable of handling matters of personal finance?" and "Is the patient capable of safely driving a car?" are more appropriate. Answers to questions such as these enable clinicians to better focus treatment, make more useful case management decisions, and generally maximize the client's overall potential. The predictive or ecological validity of neuropsychological assessment procedures clearly is enhanced by asking a specific referral question. Referral questions phrased in a dichotomous fashion are challenging as well. Referral sources often ask "Is this disorder functional or organic?" This type of question should be clarified to avoid simplistic binary classification that does not characterize most patients who are seen for neuropsychological evaluation. Instead, the referral source might ask how psychological and neuropsychological factors are affecting a client, given the client's unique strengths and weaknesses. Many of these issues can be clarified through early discussion with the referral source, leading to examination procedures that are better tailored to the client.

Diagnostic Issues

The neuropsychological examination also is affected by taxonomic issues inherent to a particular case. Although a patient's behavior and performance during an evaluation dictate the direction of further assessment, the initial examination often centers around potential diagnoses. Because of the higher incidence of dementing illnesses and depression in geriatric populations, for example, an older client being seen secondary to gradually declining cognitive status might undergo assessment procedures that thoroughly investigate the course of the deterioration and nature of onset, deficits in memory and problem solving, and issues related to affective status. Initial diagnostic questions might then generate different lines of clinical interviewing and test selection.

Record Review

In many cases, the first information a neuropsychologist receives following the referral is some element of a patient's medical history. A record review prior to formal neuropsychological evaluation tells the neuropsychologist which tests will be most appropriate and critical to the examination, which areas of a patient's history should be comprehensively investigated during the clinical interview, what rehabilitation or vocational issues might be driving the neuropsychological referral (e.g., whether the patient can benefit from further outpatient occupational therapy), and what diagnostic possibilities are most likely. A description of the initial accident or illness onset and the ensuing medical intervention are critical aspects of the medical record. The hospital emergency room report, if it exists, and admission and discharge summaries provide a concise overview of the disorder. Reports of neuroradiological procedures, such as magnetic resonance imaging, computerized tomography, and single-photon emission computed tomography, give neuropsychologists a clear understanding of the extent and localization of neurological involvement. Neuropsychologists also look for previous evaluations conducted by professionals in psychology or other disciplines. A previous neuropsychological report is helpful, and reports from speech and language pathology, social work, and other disciplines can provide invaluable information regarding cognitive or emotional status. Progress notes and the discharge summary indicate the rate of a patient's recovery and suggest what level of recovery the patient will have attained when he or she is seen by the neuropsychologist. Reports from the treating physician and individuals in other disciplines also give the neuropsychologist a better understanding of the patient's medical, social, vocational, and academic history.

Initial Interview

The interview with the patient has many objectives and may require up to 2 hr to complete. A neuropsychologist spends the first part of the interview educating the patient about the examination procedure. This discussion includes clarification of the referral process and questions to be answered by the examination; explanation of the nature of the evaluation and testing process; information about who will receive copies of the report and how findings will be used; a description of client rights, including confidentiality; a statement concerning how the client will receive feedback on his or her performance; and time to answer the client's questions.

Another primary agenda for the interview is to gather critical information that, together with the case history/medical record and formal testing data, forms the basis for diagnostic and treatment conclusions and recommendations. The qualitative findings of the interview can dramatically alter the interpretation of subsequent neuropsychological test results

(Lezak, 1983). The flexibility of the interview yields uniquely valuable information. However, by allowing the neuropsychologist to follow or reject various lines of inquiry, it can produce erroneous conclusions through "confirmatory bias." Confirmatory bias is the tendency to seek and value evidence in support of a working hypothesis while ignoring or minimizing contradictory evidence (Greenwald, Pratkanis, Leippe, & Baumgardner, 1986). Maloney and Ward (1976) suggested that the interview proceed from open-ended questions to more structured questions that clarify details or inconsistencies. Most neuropsychologists use a preprinted interview form (see Appendix B), ensuring that all relevant areas are addressed. Four areas are particularly germane to the differential diagnostic process: previous psychological and medical history, educational and vocational background, current life situation, and context of the evaluation. Information relevant to these domains assists in establishing an expected level of performance on neuropsychological tests and communicates potential premorbid conditions or influences that may have affected neuropsychological status prior to the accident or illness in question.

Like the general clinician, the neuropsychologist begins observing a client's behavior during the procedures surrounding the clinical interview, noting the client's ability to follow directions to the hospital or office, find the correct room, and arrive on time. The level of performance on these tasks provides information about the client's functional status. The neuropsychologist pursues three goals when observing a patient. First, the neuropsychologist looks for clear pathognomonic signs: Certain behaviors, such as a drooping eyelid, are hallmarks of neurological or neuropsychological dysfunction. Second, the clinician informally assesses the patient's levels of cognitive and physical impairment to make sure selected neuropsychological measures are of an appropriate difficulty level and will address the deficits in question. Finally, observation of the patient alerts the neuropsychologist to emotional and current-state factors that could adversely affect the patient's performance on neuropsychological tests.

Test Selection and Administration

To choose appropriate tests, a neuropsychologist must be familiar with the abundant array of neuropsychological instruments that are currently available. The battery selected should have ample breadth of coverage while allowing for in-depth inspection of anticipated domains of weakness, as judged by the initial referral or record review. Administration of a single test of memory and omnibus intellectual measure does not represent appropriate coverage in most cases. Conversely, using time-consuming extensive fixed batteries (e.g., the Halstead–Reitan battery) can preclude more intensive testing of the most pertinent neuropsychological domains. Use of a flexible battery approach is one solution to this dilemma (Sweet, Moberg, & Westergaard, 1996). The neuropsychologist starts using tests that are broadly sensitive to a wide array of disorders or lesion sites using a brief set of measures that are based on record review, the nature of the referral question, assumptions regarding brain–behavior relations, and the overall goal of the examination. Additional measures are then selected, on the basis of information gleaned during the clinical interview, behavioral observations made during initial patient contact, and initial test findings. Although a basic battery is generally appropriate for a range of neurological disorders, many neuropsychologists prefer disorder-specific batteries that have unique relevance and normative bases with the particular population in question. An example of such a battery is the Consortium to Establish a Registry for Alzheimer's Disease (Mirra et al., 1991), a battery used in the assessment of dementia.

Critical within the flexible approach is the notion of hypothesis testing, in which the neuropsychologist begins to answer some parts of the referral question while raising new questions and modifying initial findings. This process typically involves the use of tests that focus on qualitative aspects of a patient's performance. For example, if the examiner becomes suspicious of memory disturbance after the patient fails to recall information that was discussed during the clinical interview, he or she might then use a memory measure to reveal specific difficulties with primarily verbal material that is presented orally. Additional testing might be used to identify which aspect of memory—acquisition, storage, or retrieval—is predominantly responsible for the client's functional memory difficulties. Given the complexity of most neuropsychological tests, a lot of overlap exists within the cognitive domains being tapped by a task. For this reason, the examiner may need to vary the task demands (e.g., visual vs. auditory, verbal vs. nonverbal) in a systematic fashion to ascertain the specific element that is impaired. Three of the most commonly used means for evaluating neuropsychological capacity are the Luria Nebraska Neuropsychological Battery (LNNB; Golden, Hammeke, & Purisch, 1982), the Halstead–Reitan Neuropsychological Battery (HRNB; Macciocchi & Barth, 1996), and the Boston Process Approach (Moses & Purisch, 1997).

LNNB. The LNNB is a standardized battery of neuropsychological tasks that consists of 269 items (Form I) or 279 items (Form II). The scales that compose the LNNB evaluate motor functions, rhythm, tactile functions, visual functions, receptive and expressive speech, writing, reading, arithmetic, memory, intellectual processes, and immediate memory. Impaired performance is determined independently for each scale by comparing a patient's score for that scale with the critical level. The critical level is corrected for age and education using a specific mathematical formula.

Four levels of interpretation are available for the LNNB (Golden, Purisch, & Hammeke, 1985). The first level is aimed at determining whether brain injury is present. Delineation of a patient's functional abilities and impairments occurs at the second level. The third level targets probable causes of the patient's behavior. The fourth level involves an integrative summary of test results into a description of the patient's neuropsychological functioning.

The LNNB has clinical utility with certain populations but inadequately assesses some clinical deficits. Franzen (1989) suggested that the battery does not distinguish between average and superior levels of performance. Also, much of the battery is verbally based and does not adequately assess complex visuomotor capacity. It also may be poorly suited for the evaluation of aphasia (Crosson & Warren, 1982) or higher order cognitive disturbance (Purisch & Sbordone, 1986). Although controversy surrounds the LNNB, investigators have obtained adequate estimates of reliability and validity (Maruish, Sawicki, Franzen, & Golden, 1985).

HRNB. The HRNB is a comprehensive battery developed to reliably, validly, and completely assess the behavioral correlates of brain function (Reitan, 1986). The HRNB is composed of six categories of measures: (a) input; (b) attention, concentration, and memory; (c) verbal abilities; (d) spatial, sequential, and manipulatory abilities; (e) abstract reasoning, logical analysis, and concept formation; and (f) output (Reitan & Wolfson, 1993). The battery comprises the following tests: Category Test, Speech Sounds Perception Test, Seashore Rhythm Test, Trail Making Test (Parts A and B), Tactual Performance Test, Reitan–Klove Sensory–Perceptual Examination, Aphasia Screening Examination, and Finger Oscillation Test. The Wechsler Adult Intelligence Scale–III (WAIS–III; Wechsler, 1997a) and Minnesota Multiphasic Personality Inventory–2 (MMPI–2) frequently are administered with these tasks to establish a general level of cognitive functioning and assess psychological status.

Basic interpretive strategy for the HRNB includes five steps (Reitan & Wolfson, 1993). Initially, the neuropsychologist checks the results of hold tests (measures that are least sensitive to acquired brain dysfunction) on the WAIS–III to estimate premorbid functioning, thereby obtaining a comparative backdrop for evaluating the potential of recent cognitive decline. Next the clinician reviews summary scores from the HRNB that are known to differentiate between individuals with neurological problems and those without such conditions. The third step involves lateralizing the region of cerebral damage. The fourth step is to discern the course of the suspected lesion. Finally, the clinician synthesizes all sources of data and information to draw meaningful clinical inference about the neurological disorder.

In general, the HRNB possesses adequate reliability (Boll, 1981; Franzen, 1989). Although some studies have demonstrated solid validity, controversy concerning the HRNB's diagnostic utility continues. One concern involves the HRNB's limitations in assessing disorders of learning and memory. Indeed, Reitan (1986) suggested that in certain clinical situations it might be necessary to include supplementary tests of memory. Reitan also has suggested additional assessment of motor functioning, verbal problem solving (Reitan, 1986), and word finding in certain clinical situations (Reitan, 1972).

The Boston Process Approach. Along with the quantitative data generated by the battery of tests, neuropsychologists can derive a wealth of qualitative data from the *manner* in which a patient performs. The Boston Process Approach to neuropsychological assessment originated with the contributions of Werner (1937), who maintained that observation of task process—the manner in which a patient solves or fails a given problem—is more critical to understanding his or her cognitive status than simply noting task achievement (success or failure).

An information-processing perspective, which involves analyzing each task to fractionate the cognitive demands collectively required by the task, is critical to the process-based approach. Thus, if a patient performs poorly on a measure with multiple cognitive demands, the examiner follows up with increasingly "process-pure" tests (tests demanding only one type of cognitive ability). In this way, the clinician systematically explores and exploits the information-processing requirements of standard tests by controlling the input, processing, and output demands and directs the patient to perform increasingly process-specific measures until the exact nature of a cognitive deficit can be identified (Bauer, 1994).

With the Boston Process Approach, many of the measures present in fixed batteries can be used, or standardized tests may be modified to yield more precise or qualitative clinical data. In many cases, additional information is revealed by testing the limits. In other words, by first obtaining a valid score on a given test or item and then going beyond standardized administrative procedures, neuropsychologists can glean more information about the nature of a patient's failure. The examiner might de-emphasize time parameters, provide more structure for a task, or deconstruct the test so that only a single cognitive demand is required for success on the task. For example, the Digit Symbol subtest of the WAIS–III, given in standard fashion, requires attention, working memory, visual scanning, and a high degree of psychomotor speed. When this subtest indicates impairment, any of these factors may be deficient. Neuropsychologists can carefully manipulate single elements of the task to better isolate the deficient function. Having the individual simply copy the symbol rather than make the association between symbol or number, for instance, can provide information about the role of simple psychomotor speed. Having the patient recall which symbol was paired with which number, on the other hand, attests to the role of working memory in overall performance of the test. Careful and systematic analysis through testing of the limits can provide a clearer understanding of the extent to which a function or functional system is impaired and the impact this impairment may have on related functional systems (Cohen & Mapou, 1988).

Interpretation of Neuropsychological Information

At the most basic level, neuropsychological evaluation data can be expressed as either quantitative (numerical) or qualitative (descriptive; Lezak, 1995), and some practitioners rely exclusively on one type or the other in interpreting results and arriving at a diagnosis and recommendations. Proponents of a strictly quantitative approach often use a technician to administer tests in an attempt to isolate quantitative test data from sources of qualitative data, such as observation. Although some individuals argue for the superiority of a purely quantitative approach to decision making (Meehl, 1954; Wedding & Faust, 1989), this position has not been universally adopted by neuropsychology (Leli & Filskov, 1984). Other neuropsychologists take a clinically oriented approach that places emphasis on the quality of a patient's performance rather than on quantifying the performance and comparing it within a normative context (Christensen, 1979). Still other neuropsychologists think integration of these two components of interpretation provides the fullest interpretive picture. This approach has evolved from the work of Werner (1937), which stresses the importance of observing a client during testing to determine how a task is achieved or failed, because the same result can occur via numerous means. Kaplan (1988) further refined this process approach to neuropsychological assessment by reviewing traditionally quantitative measures to glean more qualitative or "process" information from them. Such analysis is represented in the WAIS as a Neuropsychological Instrument, or WAIS–NI, in which supplemental procedures are added to the standard WAIS to gain a more thorough understanding of how a patient successfully completes or fails a given item or subtest.

One of the biggest challenges to neuropsychologists is deciding whether a specific performance represents impairment of a given neuropsychological function. Determining the threshold for impairment often involves the concept of *deficit measurement*. To determine if a decline or deficit is present, the patient's performance is measured in one of two ways: either against (a) a population-based normative standard (normative comparison) or (b) an optimal or normal premorbid level for the individual (individual comparison). Many neuropsychologists use both comparative standards, letting the nature of the examination and the referral question determine the extent to which each standard is emphasized. For example, an evaluation to determine whether an individual is suited to a specific educational training experience or vocational arena would rely more on normative comparison, whereas an evaluation of a chemical engineer to determine the level of cognitive decline caused by a cerebrovascular accident would place emphasis on comparing the engineer's current functioning with his or her premorbid functioning. Descriptions of the two methods follow.

Normative comparison. One method of comparing a client's existing ability level in a given cognitive domain, such as attention span or visual perception, is to measure performance against a mean value within the population at large. When comparing a client's test performance with a population value, the normative population should be as demographically similar to the client as possible. Using a normative base that is similar to the client in terms of gender, ethnicity, age, and education level leads to more accurate diagnostic statements. In addition, the concept of local norms is gaining support as neuropsychologists recognize the value of comparing clients with similar individuals in the clients' own communities rather than resorting to nationally derived norms that might be unrepresentative of clients seen in given institutions or practice settings. To this end, a move is afoot to accumulate norms on healthy individuals in local communities to be used as comparative backdrops.

A second type of normative comparison uses criteria that are set somewhat arbitrarily and represent levels of function assumed to be attained by most neurologically intact individuals. Such a comparison is useful in evaluations of competency, in which a certain threshold of functioning is required. For example, the reason for the evaluation might be to determine if the client can make independent decisions regarding medical care. In this case, it is more important that the client exhibit a minimal level of capacity in a given cognitive domain that has some critical functional significance rather than be compared with a population average.

Individual comparison. Neuropsychologists often are called on to evaluate whether a patient has experienced cognitive decline. Obviously, this issue is better addressed by comparing the patient's current performance level with his or her ability prior to the onset of the injury or illness. This comparison ideally is made by contrasting current standardized test performance with performance on the same test executed prior to the onset of the neurological insult. This method, known as *direct measurement of deficit*, is powerful in revealing declines from a premorbid level of functioning.

In most cases, however, baseline neuropsychological testing is not available, and current neuropsychological data must be compared with an indirect measurement, or estimate, of the patient's premorbid level of functioning. Estimates of premorbid functioning are founded on two general sources of patient information. One method uses demographic variables—such as years of education, vocational classification, and age—that have been found to correlate with overall intellectual capacity. Using an algorithm, each variable is given a specific numeric value that is then multiplied by different mathematical constants, the results of which are ultimately summed to produce estimated Verbal, Performance, and Full Scale IQ scores. A widely used demographic-based estimate of premorbid IQ is the Barona formula (Barona, Reynolds, & Chastain, 1984), which is shown in Exhibit 6.2.

A second method for estimating premorbid functioning involves the use of current performance on particular tests that are believed to hold, or remain relatively resistant to the effects of, an acquired neurological injury or illness. Reading level, for example, appears to hold. Nelson and O'Connell (1978) used the number of errors made on the National Adult Reading Test (NART) to estimate premorbid Verbal, Performance, and Full Scale IQ. A revised version of the NART (NART–R), developed by Blair and Spreen (1989), is now available and comprises 61 irregular words that cannot be pronounced by applying simple phonetic rules (e.g., *yacht*). This presumably taps a patient's premorbid familiarity with certain words, or developmental reading level, to a greater extent than a measure that uses words with regular spellings.

Furthermore, combining demographic-based estimates with performance-derived estimates can improve the accuracy of premorbid IQ estimates. Corrigan and Berry (1991) found that the arithmetic mean of the Barona formula estimate and NART–R estimate yields a more accurate estimate of premorbid IQ than either score alone.

Using Feedback From the Neuropsychological Consult

Using the results of neuropsychological assessment to meaningfully assist a client is the essence of clinical neuropsychology. If the clinical implications of neuropsychological findings and explicit plans for intervention are not clearly

Exhibit 6.2

Calculating the Barona Formula

Demographic-based Formulae for Estimating Verbal, Performance, and Full Scale IQ scores

Estimated WAIS–R Verbal IQ =

54.23 + 0.49 (Age) + 1.92 (Sex) + 4.24 (Race) + 1.89 (Occupation) + 5.25 (Education) + 1.24 (U-R Residence)

Standard Error of Estimate = 11.79

Estimated Performance IQ =

61.58 + 0.31 (Age) + 1.09 (Sex) + 4.95 (Race) + 3.75 (Education) + 1.54 (Occupation) + 0.59 (Region)

Standard Error of Estimate = 13.25

Estimated Full Scale IQ =

54.96 + 0.47 (Age) + 1.76 (Sex) + 4.71 (Race) + 5.02 (Education) + 1.89 (Occupation) + 0.59 (Region)

Standard Error of Estimate = 12.14

Variables

Sex:
  Female = 1, Male = 2
Race:
  African-American = 1; other ethnicity = 2; White = 3
Region:
  South = 1; North Central = 2; Western = 3; Northeastern = 4
Residence:
  Rural = 1; Urban = 2
Occupation:
  Farm laborers, farm foreman, and unskilled laborers = 1
  Operative, service workers, farmers, and farm managers (semiskilled) = 2
  Not in labor force = 3
  Craftsmen and foreman (skilled workers) = 4
  Sales workers, clerical positions, managers, officials = 5
  Professional and technical = 6
Age:
  16–17 years = 1; 18–19 years = 2; 20–24 years = 3; 25–34 = 4; 35–44 = 5; 45–54 = 6; 55–64 = 7; 65–69 = 8; 70–74 = 9
Education:
  0–7 years = 1; 8 years = 2; 9–11 years = 3; 12 years = 4; 13–15 years = 5; 16 or more = 6

communicated from the neuropsychologist to the general clinician, the neuropsychological consult is little more than an academic exercise. Gaps in communication occur at both points: In some cases, neuropsychologists fail to write usable reports; in others, generalists have difficulty grasping the nuances of this specialized area. In addition, both specialists and generalists sometimes have trouble conveying findings into concrete case management strategies. This section provides general clinicians with a knowledge base by which to effectively use feedback from the neuropsychological consult.

Format of the Neuropsychological Report

The organization of neuropsychological reports follows the format of the evaluation. Usually, some variant of the shell outlined in Exhibit 6.3 is used to organize the information gathered during the record review, interview, and formal testing portions of the examination. Much of the outline is self-explanatory; some sections are described herewith in more detail.

Client identification and demographic information. This section includes basic information such as the client's name, birth date, address, hospital ID number (if appropriate), and date of testing. The section also identifies the neuropsychologist conducting the evaluation, the agency or institution in which testing was conducted, and the individual who referred the client to the neuropsychologist. A statement following the above information might suggest limits of validity for the report (e.g., 1 year) or clarify the confidential nature of the report.

Reason/circumstance for referral. Neuropsychologists often restate early in the body of the report the purpose of the evaluation, clinical decisions dependent on the findings, and questions to be answered by the report. The remainder of the report revolves around these issues.

Client presenting problems and recent history. This section includes information concerning cognitive, physical, or psychological symptoms expressed by the patient and infor-

---

Exhibit 6.3

Format of a Neuropsychological Report

    I.   Client identification and demographic information
   II.   Reason/circumstance for referral
  III.   Client presenting problem(s) and recent history
   IV.   Client background and history
        A.   Previous medical/psychiatric and family history
        B.   Developmental and educational history
        C.   Social and vocational history
        D.   Behavioral observations
    V.   Tests administered
   VI.   Test results
        A.   Overall intellectual and academic achievement
             functioning
        B.   Attention and concentration/vigilance
        C.   Learning and memory
        D.   Language
        E.   Visuospatial and visual perceptual
        F.   Sensory and motor functioning
        G.   Executive control functioning
        H.   Personality and psychosocial status
  VII.   Conclusions and recommendations

---

mation directly related to the reason for referral, such as potential etiologic factors, medical antecedents, time of onset, disease course, and pertinent neurological or radiological findings.

Client background and history. Relevant aspects of a patient's extended medical, psychiatric, family, developmental, educational, social, and vocational histories are chronicled in separate sections within the report. In deciding what to include in this section, the neuropsychologist considers what information has been provided to the reader in other reports, as a way of maximizing economy and minimizing redundancy; what information will provide a better understanding of premorbid cognitive and functional status; and what information will help the reader understand the impact of the client's impairments on his or her social, psychological, and vocational interests and lifestyle.

Behavioral observations. During the lengthy neuropsychological assessment process a neuropsychologist has ample opportunity to observe a client's appearance, style, and behavior as well as qualitative aspects of the client's cognitive functioning. Because other, more general psychological or psychiatric reports often include broad behavioral observations this section in the neuropsychological report focuses on elements of the client's behavior that are directly related to the purpose of the neuropsychological examination, particularly aspects of the client's behavior related to functional cognitive status. For example, the report should note how well the client attends to and retains test instructions, follows directions, and persists on difficult tasks. The client's response to the demands of the testing situation should be described. What is the client's reaction to success or failure on given tasks or items? What is his or her reaction to encouragement from the examiner? This section includes discussion of compensatory strategies that are demonstrated during the evaluation. Does the client bring a list of questions to ask during the interview? Does the client use a schedule book or consult with family members in an effective fashion? In this section the neuropsychologist might comment on the perceived validity of the examination process by including information about appropriate levels of cooperation and motivation on the part of the client and evidence that performance may have been affected by medication, illness, or distraction.

Test results. It is most helpful when this section is divided into subsections that deal with cognitive domains addressed by the evaluation, such as attention or memory, as opposed to subsections that simply cover the tests that were used. Subsections dealing with specific cognitive domains should reflect both quantitative and qualitative findings. To illustrate, a failure to attend to quantitative and qualitative features of performance contributes to failure to recognize non-Alzheimer's forms of cerebral atrophy (Neary & Snowden, 1991). Although general observations about a client's behavior are included in the behavioral observations section of the report, aspects of behavior that are relevant to a given cognitive domain should be included, along with quantitative data, in the subsection for that domain. For example, observations of poor impulse control or overtly concrete thinking (becoming fixed on a superficial aspect of test stimulus materials rather than the essential purpose of the task) belong in the segment of the report that covers executive control because of the implications for certain types of frontal lobe disturbance.

Many neuropsychological reports are intended for interdisciplinary audiences, so test scores should be described in an easily absorbed manner. Most professionals appreciate the use of percentiles, for example (Saling, 1994). In addition to overall score and percentile values, the report should explain the significance of score differences and provide comparisons to healthy populations (Kaufman, 1990). The issue of clinical meaning versus statistical significance is especially important with neuropsychological test findings that are assumed to have normative significance. Psychological or personality test findings are significant in neurological populations and have direct implications for interpretation of cognitive test findings.

Conclusions and recommendations. This section of the report begins with a brief review of the reason for referral, description of the patient, and short summary of relevant test findings and then focuses on answers to referral questions, diagnostic formulations, and functional implications. Conclusions should be clear to a variety of interdisciplinary specialists and should not include jargon. Information related to diagnostic conclusions should make "neuropsychological" or "neuropathologic" sense. Along with a discussion of the nature of diagnostic and functional conclusions, the neuropsychologist should indicate how confident he or she is of any such conclusions. The recommendations section of the report is sometimes formulated as bulleted points or numbered items to facilitate clarity and readability and to assist the individual responsible for implementing clinical directives. Initial recommendations often prescribe additional referrals needed to clarify the diagnosis suggested by the evaluation. Other recommendations are related to future interventions or case management. This section of the report includes information related to the client's rehabilitative, vocational, and adaptive capacities and how these functions can be improved in a real world sense.

Supplementary Contact With the Neuropsychological Consultant

In certain cases, general clinicians require additional feedback from neuropsychologists in the form of telephone contact, an addendum to the original report, or further evaluative services for the patient. For example, after the initial referral is made, a general clinician might receive new information that could assist the neuropsychologist in evaluating the client. After the evaluation is complete, the general clinician might require more information to clarify the report findings. Because of differences in communication styles, nomenclatures, or the perceived scope of the report, requested information may be absent or unclear to the referring clinician. In addition, the report content sometimes generates further questions regarding the functional or psychotherapeutic significance of examination findings. Finally, the general clinician, after working with the client for a time, might have difficulty implementing recommendations from the report and require follow-up to modify clinical interventions. Even insightful and accurate recommendations cannot anticipate all forms of behavioral response from the client.

Psychological Assessment Following the Neuropsychological Evaluation

No single test or scale assesses all aspects of psychosocial status critical for diagnosis and intervention with neurologically involved populations. In fact, acquiring a complete understanding of the complex dynamics of a social system through tests alone is impossible. Consequently, results of the neuropsychological examination sometimes signal the need for auxiliary psychological assessment aimed at selecting and implementing treatment intervention strategies. In conducting various aspects of the psychological assessment process that follows the neuropsychological evaluation—clinical interviews, observation of the client, and formal psychological tests of emotional and psychosocial functioning—the general practitioner must use clinical insight and possess a full understanding of the psychological and social impact of the patient's particular neurological condition.

Clinical interviews. According to Pasino (1979), emotional response to neurological trauma affects a patient's ability to respond to interventions and use returning skills in functional activity. Mental and psychosocial domains are critical to long-term functional outcome and community integration and are less amenable than physical impairment to today's increasingly time-limited rehabilitation efforts. An individual's views about his or her own competencies and postinjury status are paramount when planning ongoing rehabilitation efforts.

In an article describing psychosocial and neuropsychiatric care issues in individuals with human immunodeficiency virus, or HIV or acquired immune deficiency syndrome (AIDS) dementia, Flaskerud (1992) pointed out that the major psychological stress on people with AIDS is the awareness that they have a fatal disease with the potential for a rapid declining course to death, and suggests a thorough psychosocial assessment that provides a useful template for psychosocial assessment in a variety of neurodegenerative and neurological illness at large. The assessment incorporates the following topics: current distress and crisis, phase of the illness, past psychosocial history, life cycle phase, individual identity, issues of loss and grief, level of coping, and existing social support.

Talking to caregivers is also a critical component in sorting out the psychosocial status of the patient. Important differences generally exist between the accounts of patients and the accounts of caregivers concerning psychosocial changes in the patients. Accounts of cognitive functioning usually reflect wider discrepancy between patients and caregivers than ratings of physical dimensions and functional capacity, and the emotional–behavioral realm represents the area with greatest discrepancy (McKinlay & Brooks, 1984).

Formal tests and rating scales. As previously stated, valid clinical judgments concerning emotional and psychosocial features of neurological illness cannot be based solely on personality inventories such as the MMPI–2. However, some neuropsychologists administer an omnibus objective personality measure such as the MMPI–2 as the sole indicator of psychological or psychosocial status. As a result, additional formal psychological testing may be required.

Developed for use by psychologists working with medical patients, the Millon Behavioral Health Inventory (Millon, Green, & Meagher, 1979, 1982) has specific utility in neuropsychological cases because neuropsychological involvement coincides with a variety of conditions that affect the central nervous system and other systems. Because the inventory assesses health attitudes and coping styles, it can illuminate a client's cognitive and neurological status in the context of overall psychosocial and emotional functioning.

According to Garske and Thomas (1992), the Human Service Scale (HSS), developed by Kravetz (1973), is significantly correlated with the injury-severity variable of coma duration. This finding suggests that comprehensive, multidimensional psychosocial assessment is critical to defining the rehabilitation needs of the patient. The HSS is an 80-item Likert-type scale, with items presented in a multiple-choice format. It contains seven subscales that address perception of physical health, emotional security, economic security, family interaction, social involvement, economic self-esteem, and vocational self-actualization. Reliability estimates for the seven subscales range from .69 to .97. Kravetz pointed out that the factors that comprise the HSS resemble Maslow's hierarchy of human needs.

Jackson et al. (1992) examined the utility of a modified version of the Katz Adjustment Scale–Relatives Form (KAS–R). Although the KAS–R in its original form is superior to other omnibus personality measures when assessing psychosocial status following neurological injury or illness, it possesses several disadvantages. For this reason, Jackson et al. modified the KAS–R to include information comparing patient change from premorbid levels and identified a factor structure specific to a traumatic brain-injured population (rather than a psychiatric population). Factor analysis of the modified version of the KAS–R yielded 30 first-order factors under the domains of emotional–psychosocial, physical–intellectual, and psychiatric changes and 7 second-order factors identifiable as syndromes that often accompany frontal lobe injury. KAS–R items are useful in distinguishing well-adjusted and poorly adjusted patients. Also, the KAS–R is unique in its capacity to assess behavior as it occurs within the community. This feature extends the evaluation beyond the artificial, structured context of the neuropsychological assessment laboratory to functional psychosocial realms.

A significant relation exists between rehabilitation-need satisfaction and perceived self-esteem (Garske & Thomas, 1992). The Rosenberg Self-Esteem Scale (Rosenberg, 1965) is a 10-item inventory with a 4-point Likert-type scale ranging from *strongly agree* (4) to *strongly disagree* (1). The scale is widely used and demonstrates solid psychometric evidence (Prendergast & Binder, 1975).

Spilker (1990) asserted that assessing the quality of life (QOL) of clients being treated for medical or psychological disorders improves the effectiveness of treatment. Thus, QOL issues should receive formal assessment within the psychosocial realm. Despite the highly relevant nature of life quality, measurement of QOL is still in its infancy, without data to support the use of this construct as a basis for health care decisions. Because each individual defines his or her own QOL, Whiteneck (1994) recommended a composite measure of multiple factors, such as perceived health, activity level, and role satisfaction, and QOL measures should reflect the perspective of the individual rather than observations made by others.

Weitzner, Meyers, and Byrne (1996) suggested that the QOL of patients with brain tumors is most affected by the extent of tumor involvement. Bilateral tumor involvement, for example, is associated with an overall decline in QOL, impairment in physical and functional domains, and further dysfunction in family relationships and job-related satisfaction. Greater psychiatric symptomology in patients with bilateral involvement may bring about these deficits. Other factors affecting QOL in this population are poor performance status, gender, marital status, aggressiveness of the treatment regimen, and unemployment. Age and tumor grade are not related to QOL.

QOL assessment can be used as a way of monitoring the impact of an intervention or treatment on how a patient feels and functions in his or her daily life. The Quality of Life Rating (QOLR; Allen, Huebner, Inman, Turpin, & Gust, 1997) represents a psychometrically solid, norm-based instrument that measures a number of life domains in neurologically involved populations. The QOLR contains 20 brief question stems that are responded to in a Likert fashion. These items form five basic factors that resemble both Maslow's hierarchy of needs (Maslow, 1970) and the World Health Organization's conceptualization of components that make up quality of life (World Health Organization Quality of Life Group, 1996). Data have been collected for specific medical and neurological populations, including traumatic brain injury and geriatric medical patients. Appendix D shows the QOLR.

Integrating Neuropsychological Assessment and Psychological Assessment

Various formal measures provide a snapshot of current psychological status and difficulties; however, they do not adequately address such vital areas as the individual's change from premorbid style, available coping mechanisms, insight into and reaction to recent cognitive and physical impairment, level of family distress and competency to assist the patient during recovery, or availability of social support and resources in general. Accordingly, a multitrait, multimethod approach should be used to assess the psychosocial and cognitive sequelae that follow neurological disease or injury. For example, having relatives provide comparative ratings of the patient's pre- and postillness psychosocial functioning not only sheds light on the contribution of neuropathology and premorbid personality variables but also alerts clinicians to patient behaviors that family members might view as new and disturbing. Such information exponentially adds to clinicians' understanding of family dynamics, tolerance of patient behaviors and, ultimately, the potential for successful independent functioning and social and community reintegration.

Conclusion

A thorough understanding of the neuropsychological evaluation process is essential for making an appropriate referral for specialized assessment. Without such an understanding, clients may be unnecessarily triaged to a multitude of professionals who add nothing to the client's diagnosis or treatment needs. Furthermore, clinicians who are enlightened about the nature of specialized services are better able to make recommendations to neuropsychologists or incorporate feedback from the neuropsychological assessment into general treatment strategies.

Additional Reading

Clinician's Guide to Neuropsychological Assessment (2nd ed., Vanderploeg, 2000) provides the reader with information concerning a number of current issues and topics related to neuropsychological diagnosis, application of test findings, and other topics relevant to clinical practice. A well-organized and practical introduction to administration, scoring, and interpretation of specific neuropsychological tests is *A Compendium of Neuropsychological Tests: Administration, Norms, and Commentary* (2nd ed., Spreen & Strauss, 1998). Almost encyclopedic in nature, *Neuropsychological Assessment* (3rd ed., Lezak, 1995) provides comprehensive coverage of an array of cognitive and neuropsychological tests.

7

Psychological Intervention With the Neuropsychologically Involved Client

The history of psychotherapeutically treating people who have brain damage evolved as a natural junction of neuropsychology and psychotherapy (Miller, 1997). Despite the increasing integration of those disciplines, along with others, such as rehabilitation psychology and abnormal psychology, however, dichotomous thinking continues to impede the valuing of psychotherapy for neuropsychologically involved individuals. The simplistic view that psychological symptoms are either "organic" or "functional" continues to attenuate the efficacy and value that accompany appropriately delivered psychotherapeutic services for individuals with brain damage. Also, a mindset persists that every person who has sustained a brain injury is too cognitively impaired to benefit from verbal therapy. This perspective is often upheld regardless of the severity of the neurological accident or illness, the cerebral reserve capacity of the client, or the mode or scope of the intended psychotherapeutic services. Langer (1992) identified the central goal of psychotherapy as effecting a beneficial change in the client through verbal or symbolic interaction. This broad objective seems appropriate for a variety of clinical problems, yet many therapists continue to view psychological issues accompanying neurological etiologies as being outside this purview.

Using Neuropsychological Findings in Treatment Planning

The ultimate goal of neuropsychological assessment is an improvement in the overall cognitive, functional, or psychological status of an individual who has experienced neurological compromise. To this end, at least five specific domains of intervention should be addressed through the evaluation and subsequent treatment by the clinician. These domains are psychological intervention (which is discussed in the ensuing sections of this chapter), diagnosis and prognosis, medical intervention, case management, and ecological or functional intervention. In other words, treatment planning is organized around the same categories as the initial referral for neuropsychological assessment, as discussed in chapter 6.

Diagnosis and Prognosis

Neuropsychological evaluation can clarify unresolved diagnostic dilemmas. Following the neuropsychological examination, however, the general clinician may face new difficulties related to the patient's or family's response to the clearer diagnostic or prognostic picture. Although neuropsychologists often discuss pragmatic implications of a diagnosis, they usually do not deal with all aspects of a patient's or family's long-term psychological reaction and adjustment to the disorder and its real world consequences. Perhaps the most important aspect of the general clinician's role at this stage is an overall knowledge of the disorder and the manner in which the disorder will affect the patient's psychological, social, functional, and quality-of-life status. In addition, the clinician should have a compendium of community resources and support groups for potential client or family referral. Finally, the clinician should have a collection of bibliotherapeutic references covering a range of neurological disorders that can be loaned to the family as background reading. Providing families with ongoing information appropriate to their evolving stages of reaction to diagnosis is paramount.

Medical Intervention

Psychological symptoms are not always best explained psychologically; mental and emotional changes commonly associated with adaptive functioning problems can result from neurological or medical dysfunction. Ideally, individuals are formally evaluated and "cleared" medically before seeking psychological services. When this does not occur, issues of clinical assessment become more complicated. For example, a client's depression may be the result of a job failure, or loss of a significant other, or it may be due to a brain tumor or hormonal dysregulation. Just as a person may inappropriately seek the care of a physician when the disorder is psychological, individuals with physical disease and injury sometimes look for solutions from psychotherapy. Indeed, it has been suggested that at least 10% of people seen for psychological symptoms are subsequently found to have causative or contributing organic disease (Taylor, 1990).

A general clinician may become aware that medical factors are producing what was initially perceived as psychological distress and symptomology only after a neuropsychological referral. In continuing treatment, the general clinician should become involved with the patient's medical circumstances. When the neuropsychological evaluation suggests additional medical consultation, the clinician can assist the client with arranging subsequent medical referrals. The clinician may be required to follow up with medical professionals after consultation services are rendered as a way of tracking the client's medical compliance and ongoing response to such interventions. Because the clinician may be in a more enduring professional relationship with the client than the physician is, the clinician may be able to observe symptom patterns and responses to medical intervention more consistently. This allows the clinician to provide medical specialists with information about the client's response to treatment that can result in improved treatment efficacy.

Case Management

Subsequent to gaining a clear understanding of the origin and nature of symptoms and referring the client to appropriate medical services, the clinician should turn his or her attention to other case management efforts that will assist the client. Because many neurological conditions have less than obvious physical signs, clients can miss out on pertinent social support systems. Therefore, clinicians should familiarize themselves with local resources, such as the Office of Disability Determination and Department of Vocational Rehabilitation, as well as state organizations that assist individuals who have specific neurological conditions. Depending on the patient's stage of recovery, it may be appropriate to pursue forms of rehabilitation not yet received. Many rehabilitation facilities have community reintegration programs that deal with the difficulties neurological patients face postacutely as they resume roles within family, social, and vocational settings. Relatively higher functioning people are retrained in such activities as parenting and performing household tasks, interviewing for jobs, associating with coworkers, and pursuing recreational or volunteer interests. The clinician also may act as an advocate as the client attempts to obtain services or resources. For example, clients who have sustained physical as well as cognitive impairments and require assistive devices or prostheses may need help engaging social service mechanisms that provide such resources. Associations that support patients with major neurological conditions are listed in Appendix E.

Ecological or Functional Intervention

Ecological and functional intervention, although at times basic, is of tremendous practical benefit to the client. Intervention may consist of working with the client's spouse or family in setting up a user-friendly home environment that targets safety and mechanisms to compensate for cognitive deficits. Educating the family about using reminders and checklists and posting easily understood lists of commonly used or emergency contacts or telephone numbers goes a long way toward improving the client's functioning within the home. Direct work with the client regarding ways to compensate for cognitive difficulties is invaluable. Teaching the skills necessary to use an alarm device and a memory notebook, for example, has significant functional value and strong generalizability to the client's real life. Context-specific environmental or behavioral interventions may require clinicians to assess vocational or recreational domains and develop strategies or aides that accommodate clients' cognitive impairments.

Influence of Cognitive Impairment on the Psychotherapeutic Process

Given the combination of diffuse cognitive deficits (e.g., slowed information processing) and focal cognitive deficits (e.g., impaired verbal attention) that can follow central nervous system damage, flexibility is a must throughout the psychotherapeutic process. The scope and nature of psychological services for the neurological patient should stem from continual appraisal, understanding, and responsiveness on the part of the therapist. The clinician should consider the changing symptoms that accompany recovery and vary the manner in which psychotherapeutic services are delivered. Intervention should address in a comprehensive and well-integrated fashion the cognitive, behavioral, psychological-existential, and social aspects of distress.

The first step for the clinician is to identify the sensory–perceptual, attentional, linguistic, memory, and reasoning or planning deficits that could prevent the delivery of effective psychological treatment. These deficits represent the most basic level of potential obstacles for the therapist. Because of these obstacles, the integration of psychotherapeutic services with cognitive rehabilitation therapy (CRT) is critical (Laatsch, 1999). Most broadly, cognitive rehabilitation involves providing activities or interventions that improve patients' cognitive abilities and helps them conceptualize their difficulties while training them to compensate (Klonoff, O'Brien, Prigatano, Chiapello, & Cunningham, 1989).

It is crucial for the success of both cognitive rehabilitation and psychotherapeutic services that integration of the two take place. Although some degree of integration is usually required in all work with neurological clients, the level of integration varies depending on a client's degree of neuro-psychological impairment, the client's specific needs, and the overall goal(s) of the therapeutic process. Laatsch (1996) pos-ited three levels of integration to assist clinicians in concep-tualizing the degree of CRT required to maximize the psy-chotherapeutic benefit: casual integration of CRT techniques in psychotherapy, moderate integration of CRT techniques in psychotherapy, and alternation of CRT with psychotherapy. The casual integration of CRT involves addressing a specific psychotherapeutic process (e.g., mild expressive language deficit) intermittently during psychotherapy. Moderate inte-gration requires some application of CRT within every ther-apy session. This scenario provides a challenging yet safe context for the client to address psychological issues affected by residual neuropsychological impairment. Alternating CRT and psychotherapy is effective with severely impaired clients who require greater environmental structure. Entire sessions dedicated to CRT are alternated with psychotherapeutic ses-sions.

Integrated CRT sessions enhance psychotherapy in several ways. They provide the therapist with a fuller understanding of how cognitive deficits act on the efficacy of therapy. They help identify neuropsychological deficits that continue to im-pair the client's social or functional capacity in daily living. Finally, they provide opportunities for the client to identify cognitive limitations and for the clinician to aid the client in compensating for such difficulties.

Strategies for Circumventing Common Cognitive Deficits in Psychotherapy

It is incumbent on the general clinician to determine if he or she is competent and amenable to effectively treat a client with neurological impairment. To effectively work with cognitively involved clients it is often critical to modify the scope, approach, or strategies used in psychotherapy. Issues of attention, memory, and language are critical to the clinical process and retention of therapeutic material. A number of strategies for dealing with the cognitive difficulties seen in this population are discussed next.

Attention

For successful psychological intervention, a client must be able to attend to and understand verbal material or therapeutic dialogue as it unfolds within a session. Clinicians can use several strategies to help neurologically impaired clients stay focused. Early in treatment, the therapist should establish a contract or predefined set of rules for refocusing the discussion if a session becomes derailed because of the client's inattention or decreased self-monitoring. The therapist and client should agree on a prompt or cue phrase, such as "Let's get back on track," to regain focus within the session. At the outset of each session, the therapist should present a limited number of topics or themes to be covered in the session; providing the client with a written list of these topics strengthens this strategy. The client will find it easier to retain the topical thread of a discussion if the therapist avoids long, complex sentences and dialogue. The patient's risk of becoming lost also can be reduced if the therapist pauses frequently while presenting therapeutic material or during dialogue to allow the client to mentally review the previous 5 min of the session.

Memory

As Bennett (1989) suggested, it is difficult to achieve a cumulative effect if memory deficits prohibit a client from retaining the conclusions, insights, or context of even a single session. Three aspects of memory dysfunction are most germane to the success of psychotherapeutic intervention: working memory, long-term memory, and meta-memory.

According to Baddeley (1986), *working memory* is the limited, temporary store where new information is held while it is manipulated in a meaningful way to solve a current problem. For example, retaining the details of a math story problem while trying to solve the problem uses the working memory. Working memory is subserved primarily by the prefrontal cortex.

Strategies that reduce the deleterious impact of working memory failure center around the encoding of therapeutic material. Frequently rehearsing verbal information is a basic tactic for improving working memory. Another is grouping similar psychotherapeutic topics or goals, which reduces the volume of material that must be held in the working memory. The therapist also should regulate the rate at which verbal information is presented.

In general, long-term memory involves memories measuring several minutes or longer. Impairment results from deficiency in any of the three stages of the long-term memory process: acquisition, storage, and retrieval. Long-term memory deficits hinder the client's use of therapeutic insights and suggestions and thwart therapeutic gains, as the client is unable to build cumulatively on previous therapeutic work or retrieve strategies for dealing with challenges that arise in his or her daily environment. Neuropsychological evaluation can identify which stage or stages of the long-term memory process are affected and, thereby, are most responsible for inefficient retention of therapeutic information.

Strategies to assist a client who experiences difficulty with long-term memory include instructing the client in ways to more effectively use symbolism (Lewis & Langer, 1994) and teaching the client methods for generating visual images when trying to encode verbal material. Teaching methods for generating visual images is particularly important when working with patients who have sustained dominant-hemisphere injuries that diminish verbal memory. Such individuals may have complete sparing of the right temporal region and thus be capable of forming visual memories. Other mnemonic strategies also may be helpful. For example, the therapist can assign a letter of the alphabet to each goal of therapy in such a way that the letters form a simple acronym.

Meta-memory is the aspect of cognition that monitors one's memory capacity. A person uses meta-memory when deciding which strategies to use to retain new information and what level of attention to direct toward new information. Meta-memory is often described as the component that "reminds us to remember."

The essential intervention for deficits in meta-memory is to help the client recognize and monitor his or her own limitations. Such an awareness motivates the client to learn and use compensatory strategies and devices, the most critical of which is the *memory notebook* (see Table 7.1). The memory notebook fosters organization and provides a method for rehearsal of treatment information. The client can use the notebook as a journal to record therapeutic highlights and the changing goals of psychotherapy and to record scheduled appointments, homework assignments, and topics covered in sessions. The client also can track important personal or family events, medication schedules, daily tasks, and vocational information. By reducing reliance on others, the memory notebook gives clients a greater sense of independence and can alleviate marital or familial stress. Because individuals with impaired meta-memory miss out on being "reminded to remember," results improve dramatically when the memory notebook is coupled with an alarm device such as that found on a digital wristwatch. The alarm prompts the client to check his or her memory notebook and perform necessary tasks in a timely fashion. Guided by the alarm, many individuals with brain damage use the notebook effectively and consistently.

Language

Given the highly verbal nature of much psychotherapeutic intervention, language deficits can seriously diminish its effectiveness. Declines in communication function usually result from left-hemisphere injuries or lesions, but right-hemisphere damage too can reduce communication abilities.

Table 7.1

Memory Notebook

Section	Description
Orientation	Contains information that is used daily to assist the client in establishing personal context. It includes personal information (e.g., Social Security number, current address) and may include a brief description of the nature and date of the injury or illness or information relevant to the current treatment setting (e.g., name of primary therapist, map of the ward or unit). This section also can include a small calendar of the year that can be checked off to orient the client to the specific date or day of the week.
Weekly schedule	Allows the client to note important dates or appointment times on a weekly schedule. Inclusion of a calendar that allows the client to plan events 2–3 months ahead also is useful.
To-do list	Allows the client to note all tasks, rehabilitation or therapeutic homework, and telephone calls that need to be accomplished during the day or week. A checklist format facilitates consistent monitoring of tasks to be completed.
Treatment summary	Assists the client in reviewing ongoing therapeutic issues, nature of group interaction, and clinical progress. A brief entry should follow each individual or group session or meeting.
Personal contacts and resources	Includes the names of clinical staff; directions to commonly frequented businesses or locations; and telephone numbers for community resources, support services, and friends and family.

Note. From *Introduction to Cognitive Rehabilitation: Theory and Practice* (p. 161) by M. M. Sohlberg and C. A. Mateer, 1989, New York: Guilford Press. Copyright 1989 by Guilford Press. Reprinted by permission.

Left-hemisphere syndromes may produce significant declines in the comprehension or expression of spoken language as well as deficits in linguistic symbol interpretation and manipulation that manifest as difficulties in reading, written expression, and certain aspects of arithmetic. Although many clients gradually regain functional or conversational language, deficits in word finding remain even years after the injury or illness. Right-hemisphere language problems more often involve an inability to process nonverbal elements of communication, such as poor interpretation of the emotional or connotative aspects of speech (e.g., tone of voice, facial expression, body posture, and gestures). Comprehending nonverbal elements of communication is primarily mediated by posterior nondominant hemisphere injuries, whereas conveying nonverbal elements of communication is a primary task of more anterior regions of the right frontal region.

Therapy for clients who have severe language disorders, such as aphasia, should be substantially modified in scope, pace, style, and content. It is critical to acquire a rich understanding of the client's formal speech and language diagnosis, strengths and weaknesses, and modes of most effective communication. Direct consultation with a speech therapist can provide this information. Pragmatic strategies that can strengthen therapeutic work depend on the nature of a client's language deficits. Clients who experience difficulty with motor speech (e.g., dysarthria) or expressive language (e.g., Broca's aphasia) may find that journaling, including doing written homework, helps them form thoughts or ideas without being hindered by expressive difficulties or word-finding problems. Because some clients have difficulty with syntactical aspects of speech, such as double negatives and inverted commands (Bracy, 1994), therapists should carefully craft therapeutic statements and ask clients to restate issues in their own words (Laatsch, 1999). Having clients summarize main topics or issues raised during a session and informing clients of the proposed focus of the next scheduled session can clarify breaches of communication and assist recall.

Clients with more extreme expressive communication deficits may benefit from visual analogs in which they place their own emotional reactions on a continuum that uses line drawings of facial expressions representing various moods (e.g., happy–sad).

Executive Control

Clients manifesting deficits in motivation, initiation of behavior, abstract reasoning, insight, planning, problem solving, or impulse control can present the most challenging situations. Many clients with medial prefrontal involvement demonstrate a paucity of productive behavior and action in general (Cummings, 1993). For this reason, structure-, goal-, and action-based therapeutic strategies are required. In addition, the significance of current behavioral problems should be emphasized to help the client see the importance of productive therapeutic work. For example, discussing the impact of negative behaviors on family members or a significant other can increase the client's motivation for treatment. When motivation for treatment is compromised by decreased awareness or insight that a problem exists, the use of video technology makes abstract issues of therapy more salient for the client. Videotaping group settings reveals issues related to social interaction that a brain-injured client might not have recognized just from the subtle reactions of people in natural social situations. Modeling of desired behavior is important, too. Combining videotape technology, which shows objective and salient examples of behaviors to be targeted for treatment, with modeling makes it easier for the client to learn new responses or behaviors. Additional structuring and rule setting within the context of therapy may be required for patients who have sustained orbital frontal damage and, therefore, experience increased impulsivity and reduced self-regulatory capacities.

Treating Behavioral and Psychological Impairments That Follow Brain Damage

Addressing the cognitive deficits a client brings to psychotherapeutic treatment is necessary, but it is not sufficient in ameliorating the patient's behavioral and psychological difficulties. As O'Hara (1988) stated, rehabilitation services that focus on cognitive abilities to the neglect of emotional or personality factors not only hinder the full range of adaptive coping but also fail to help clients redefine and integrate a new view of self.

Small (1980) suggested two major principles of psychotherapy involving clients who have brain damage. First, all clients with brain damage should not be capriciously classified as identical. Patients not only arrive in therapy with diverse educational, cultural, familial, and vocational backgrounds, but they also have distinct levels of premorbid intellectual functioning and personality styles. Also, the magnitude and constellation of patients' cognitive deficits vary depending on the etiology, severity, and localization of neuropathology. Second, treatment of a patient with brain damage requires a multimodal strategy in which issues related to altered cognition, emotion, and behavior are addressed comprehensively and actively. Because of the multifaceted nature of the problems to be addressed, the psychotherapeutic approach must be multidimensional and may include cognitive rehabilitation therapy, remedial instruction, pharmacological intervention, and environmental restructuring. The therapist may feel compelled to enlist a greater array of therapy modalities as well.

Critical Impairments

Critical psychological or behavioral issues that emerge at a high frequency following brain damage are irritability and aggression; awareness and denial; alcohol abuse; rigidity, concrete thinking, and resistance to psychotherapy; and existential issues.

Irritability and aggression. During the early stage of recovery, many moderately or severely brain-injured patients display generalized agitation or irritability in addition to decreased thresholds for frustration or overstimulation. In general, much of this agitation lacks a purposeful, organized nature. The patient simply reacts to stimuli he or she finds momentarily aversive. In many cases, this behavior abates over a period of several days or weeks.

Patients who have sustained significant damage to certain aspects of the frontal cortex may exhibit longer lasting, or even chronic, changes in their levels of aggressiveness. It is presumed that the generalized damage brought on by the trauma impairs the neural systems (e.g., frontal lobe structures) that inhibit or regulate emotional reactions (Mattson & Levin, 1990). Although premorbid personality characteristics can increase a patient's potential for aggressive acting out, even patients with no history of violence or aggression can manifest a decreased ability to inhibit aggressive impulses as a result of damage to the orbital region of the frontal cortex. Treating chronic forms of aggressiveness may require pharmacological and behavioral intervention. Eames (1988) advised that isolated use of either medication or behavioral management is inadequate to treat dyscontrol behaviors following brain injury. For this reason, it is important to work closely with the attending neurologist or physiatrist to achieve the optimal combination of medication and behavioral intervention. Carberry (1983) suggested the following guidelines for working with such clients.

- ☐ Develop a plan with the client that allows him or her as much input as possible.
- ☐ Understand the major belief systems of the client.
- ☐ Avoid power struggles or battles of will with the client.
- ☐ Reinforce the client's positive comments and behavior and ignore negative, attention-seeking comments and complaints.
- ☐ Involve the client in small steps aimed at making him or her feel less helpless.
- ☐ Use reframing of problems as a way to defuse anger, resistance, or negativism.
- ☐ In conversation with the client, avoid topics of resistance and negativism; instead, try to draw out the client's positive interests and concerns.
- ☐ When appropriate, use paradoxical techniques that consist of going with the resistance rather than using counter-retaliatory techniques.

Awareness and denial. Diminished insight and awareness of self are common sequelae of certain neurological illnesses, and the origins of such disturbances are manifold. Langer (1999) identified the tripartite model of the rehabilitation program at New York University as a useful way to categorize awareness difficulties demonstrated by patients. The three levels of awareness difficulties described by this model are *information*, *implication*, and *integration*. With awareness difficulties at the information level, patients have problems perceiving information about their disorders and can even be completely unaware of any impairment (*anosagnosia*). Difficulty understanding medical information and material related to the diagnosed condition also is classified as reduced awareness at the information level. Impaired awareness at the implication level occurs when patients perceive information but are incapable of appreciating the implications or long-term consequences of their conditions, deficits, or life situations. Awareness difficulty at the level of integration is seen in clients who accurately perceive their conditions and are aware of the implications but are unable to absorb emotionally the gravity or meaning of their situations. Defense mechanisms such as denial may appear when deficits of awareness occur at the integration level.

To effectively treat an individual with a neurological condition that affects self-awareness it is critical to clarify the etiology of the awareness deficit. Assigning such a deficit to premorbid background or capacity of understanding, a frank anosagnosia, general cognitive impairment brought on by the injury, or functional or emotional processes related to psychological stress is necessary before choosing an appropriate treatment. Clinical information can be gleaned by informally asking a client about the nature of the condition for which he or she is being treated; past medical history; the types of intervention or rehabilitation for the disorder he or she has received; and the cognitive, physical, and psychological consequences of the disease or neurological insult. The clinician also may ask about the client's understanding of prognostic expectations, goals for treatment, and functional potential. Formal awareness measures can be used as well to comprehensively assess the client's ability for introspection and self-appraisal (Simon et al., 1991).

Intervention varies, depending on the origins of clients' awareness difficulties. If a neurogenic cause predominates, the clinician may construct a cognitive framework that allows the client to gradually assimilate the nature, consequences, and long-term implications of his or her condition and functional capacity. In addition to capitalizing on spontaneous neurological recovery and providing general cognitive rehabilitation, the therapist may engage the client in therapeutic tasks and dialogue that require him or her to take on the abstract attitude (K. Goldstein, 1944). Examples of such tasks are imagining future events or life challenges or viewing oneself as outside observers might. The content of these therapeutic maneuvers can increasingly focus on issues central to the client's condition, recovery, and life situation. When awareness is reduced because of minimization or denial on the part of the client, other considerations are warranted. First, such denial may be protective and adaptive during the earliest phases of recovery as it allows the client to approach the catastrophic event and acquire other adaptive coping strategies at a reasonable pace. In addition, it may be desirable to delay the full impact of a client's reality while he or she undergoes the most intensive segment of the recovery and rehabilitation process. Finally, a deferred approach to awareness often permits a time early in treatment to build the therapeutic relationship.

Alcohol abuse. The neuropathologic effects of alcohol are widespread and include cell death, loss of dendritic branching, decreased synaptic efficiency of existing neurons, ventricular enlargement, meningeal thickening, and increased embolization (Altura & Altura, 1984). These neuropathologic consequences are brought on by direct toxic effects on the nervous system, indirect effects (e.g., malnutrition in chronic alcoholism), and effects related to withdrawal from alcohol.

Cognitive impairments secondary to alcohol abuse fall into one of three diagnostic categories: Korsakoff's syndrome, alcohol dementia, or subclinical impairment. Korsakoff's syndrome, the most severe form of alcohol-related cognitive decline, is less common than the other two categories. *Korsakoff's syndrome* refers to the chronic residual symptoms of Wernicke's encephalopathy, which most typically are (a) a severe anterograde amnesia dating from near the time of illness onset and (b) *confabulation*, the invention of details about past events to disguise an inability to remember (Butters, 1985). Although deficiencies in visuospatial and executive control functioning occur, severe amnesia characterizes the disease. Historically, confabulation was thought to be a hallmark of Korsakoff's. It now appears that this feature of the disorder is not universal and, if present, occurs early in the course of the disease. It is rare to see confabulation in patients who have had Korsakoff's for a period of 5 years or longer (Butters & Cermak, 1980). Impairments that make patients with Korsakoff's syndrome difficult to treat include poor motivation, deficits in new learning, memory impairment, and affective changes and difficulties with insight and planning (Flores, 1988).

Other individuals do not manifest the severe amnesia seen in Korsakoff's but do display significant memory impairment. When such amnesic disturbance is coupled with impairment in a second domain, such as visual perception or abstraction, the individual may meet criteria for *alcoholic dementia*. In general, neuropsychological test batteries that load heavily on visuospatial abilities, memory, abstract reasoning, and cognitive flexibility are most sensitive to the condition. It is speculated that this constellation of deficits is related specifically to changes in physiologic function of the frontal lobes (Kessler et al., 1984).

A third group of alcohol-abusing individuals displays an even more diverse array of cognitive symptoms, none of which are of the magnitude seen in Korsakoff's or alcoholic dementia. This subtle symptom pattern is frequently accompanied by an average intellectual level and uncompromised verbal skills (Hesselbrock, Weidenman, & Reed, 1985). Collectively, these issues cloud the diagnostic picture, often allowing clients who "talk a good game" to avoid formal assessment, diagnosis, and treatment of cognitive deficits (Flores, 1988).

The problems caused by alcohol abuse can be magnified by concomitant use of other drugs. One of the most common drugs taken with alcohol is cannabis. Attention, psychomotor speed, and short-term memory are most vulnerable to the effects of cannabis (Pope, Gruber, & Yurgelun-Todd, 1995). For reasons that are currently unclear, the also-popular combination of alcohol and cocaine represents a volatile pairing in terms of neurocognitive sequelae.

Cleaveland and Denier (1998) investigated the cognitive functioning of a group of alcohol and other drug abusers presenting for treatment. This group displayed attention/concentration capacities that were better than only 38% of the general population. As an average, they recalled only five digits as opposed to the typical seven for digit span. Verbal comprehension, which was assessed using only a vocabulary measure, suggested that the group was performing near the 31st percentile of the normative sample. Verbal memory reflected considerable loss of material even during a brief 5-min delay, as patients retained only 57% of the information originally presented to them. It is interesting that abstraction scores for the group were within normal limits (46th percentile) as measured by the Shipley Abstraction Scale.

In addition to the neuropathologic effects brought on by alcohol abuse alone, neuropsychological issues related to the comorbidity of alcohol use and traumatic brain injury (TBI) are notable (Alterman & Tarter, 1985). The most frequently cited and best established predisposing factor in head trauma is alcohol use prior to injury (Sparadeo & Gill, 1989). Acute use of alcohol and other drugs prior to head trauma is well established, and chronic substance abuse is prevalent in individuals sustaining head injuries. In fact, about half of head trauma patients have previous histories of alcohol abuse, according to Hillbom and Holm (1986). Moreover, alcohol abuse among individuals who have pre-injury patterns of abuse often continues following trauma. The National Head Injury Foundation (1988) found that approximately 40% of patients in postacute rehabilitation facilities had moderate to severe problems with alcohol abuse.

The incidence of substance abuse in patients with brain

injuries is estimated to be in the range of 50%–78%. Several factors help explain this relation. Some personality traits may be related to both high-risk behavior, and therefore greater risk of trauma, and a predisposition for substance abuse. The reduction in cognitive capacity and reaction time produced by the sedative effect of alcohol naturally leads to greater risk of motor vehicle accidents and other neurological injuries. The psychological distress and existential crises that follow significant neurological disability can prompt self-medication. Deficits in planning, judgment, problem solving, and impulse control may hamper patients' abilities to deal with situations that lead to substance abuse or to make logical choices to remain sober. Finally, substance abuse can independently produce neuropathologic changes that substantially impair cognitive capacities.

Traditional rehabilitation facilities often fail to incorporate substance abuse treatment into head injury rehabilitation programs. Conversely, customary alcohol and drug treatment programs require relatively intact functioning within the neuropsychological domains of attention–concentration, memory, abstract reasoning, and problem solving. Because of these inadequacies in treating this population, general clinicians are frequently approached to provide services for cognitively impaired clients who require substance-abuse treatment. To accommodate this need, Langley (1995) developed a program called *Skills Based Substance Abuse Prevention Counseling* that is designed to better manage the alcohol-related problems of individuals who have sustained TBIs. In the program, clients actively rehearse cognitive and coping skills rather than being only passively exposed to psychoeducational material about substance abuse. Awareness deficits are approached by increasing the client's problem-recognition capacity, improving self-monitoring abilities, and using strategies that are less dependent on self-awareness for successful implementation. Difficulties in impulse control are treated aggressively because of the increased sensitivity many brain-injured patients have to stimuli associated with their drugs of choice. Specific interventions include attempts to increase behavioral control through cue exposure and response prevention.

Rigidity, concrete thinking, and resistance to psychotherapy. Rigid thinking is one of the most common impasses to psychotherapeutic success with cognitively impaired clients. The term *rigidity* often is used to describe an individual who is cognitively or behaviorally inflexible. The rigid client is firmly entrenched in his or her existing attitudinal or behavioral patterns and unwilling to explore alternative opinions or perspectives. In some cases, the quality or content of a client's rigidity represents an extreme form of opinions or perspectives originally held by the individual prior to sustaining the neurological insult. The magnitude and pervasiveness of cognitive rigidity should be thoroughly assessed —through clinical interview or formal neuropsychological testing—prior to enrolling the client in any psychotherapeutic experience. If a client exhibits only mild to moderate levels of rigidity that do not permeate all aspects of his or her life, the clinician may eventually approach those attitudes by first addressing less tightly held beliefs.

Concrete thinking, which is related to rigidity, is a more generalized cognitive deficit that hinders the client in taking the abstract attitude. Concrete thinking hampers the therapeutic process by limiting the use of metaphorical language, insight, and other cognitive therapeutic approaches. Miller (1993) suggested that encouraging the generation of alternative choices or ideas can engender greater flexibility and less egocentric thinking on the part of the client.

Beyond the rigidity or cognitive inflexibility many clients display is *conscious* resistance to psychotherapeutic change. Lewis and Rosenberg (1990) proposed that many individuals with brain injury view psychotherapy as a threat to the relative safety of dependency. With disability brought on by neurological impairment, clients may receive significant support and assistance from others, exempting them from their original social, familial, and vocational roles. The client may believe that improved functioning and subsequent autonomy brought about through psychotherapy will lead to decreased social support and assistance, and even abandonment.

Existential issues. Clients who are less impaired and those further into the recovery process may experience existential struggles. Deficits in awareness and insight might preclude feelings of loss during the months immediately following onset of the injury or illness, but many clients exhibit increases in dysphoric symptoms as they become capable of accurately evaluating the catastrophic implications of their conditions. The issue of personal loss is uniquely experienced by individuals who have sustained neurological damage: Although the loss of a material item or a loved one can produce enormous grief, such scenarios may be less threatening to an individual's sense of self than the dramatic changes to cognitive capacity, behavioral style, and functional independence that follow neurological insult. Margolis (1993) advocated an approach in which the client's sense of self is fostered by identifying personal characteristics that remain following the brain injury. In addition, exploring previous losses may help the client interpret the current loss and prompt him or her to use coping strategies that were effective following those previous losses. Finally, therapists may help clients express and accurately interpret feelings of anger and frustration related to their sense of loss. Normalizing these responses is critical, as many brain-injured patients mistakenly believe that such emotions are yet another indication of their own impulse-control difficulties.

Meaningfulness and hopelessness also may emerge as critical existential issues. The impact that neurological illness has on cognitive abilities and the realms of life that require such abilities can be devastating and can alter a client's view of what is meaningful. Although vocational capacity often is viewed as the primary domain lost as a result of cognitive decline, interpersonal and recreational roles undergo equally dramatic changes, which can affect quality of life to an even greater degree. Previously high-functioning individuals may have placed great import on accomplishment and achievement. Faced with substantial cognitive limitations, they may be unable to envision the resumption of the social and vocational activities that fueled their self-esteem. Such beliefs can lead to helplessness that may be further supported, albeit inadvertently, by a spouse or family member attempting to protect the patient from additional risk or failure.

Issues of isolation and social alienation follow brain injury when individuals sustain deficits in social skills that lead to losses of previously enriching social relationships. Such losses can amplify feelings of decreased self-worth, leading to an even greater lack of confidence and an unwillingness to risk further social rejection and alienation from peers and potential dating partners.

In general, the sense of human frailty and mortality is heightened as a result of the life-threatening nature of acute neurological insult. For some patients, this produces learned helplessness and apathy. Other individuals view this increased urgency as an opportunity to embrace life to a fuller extent.

Case Example

Mrs. T, age 44 and White, has 17 years of formal education. She is the mother of two children (ages 17 and 20). She has a master's degree in business administration and worked as an upper level manager in the computer industry. She was referred for follow-up psychotherapeutic services related to depression, decreased self-esteem, and psychosocial and functional declines following a cerebrovascular accident (CVA) that occurred in 1993.

According to the patient and the medical record, Mrs. T had experienced swallowing difficulties as well as resolving hemiparesis of the left upper and lower extremities following her CVA. At the time of the CVA, Mrs. T simply thought her hands had cramped but later noticed some numbness in her lips, which prompted her to seek medical attention. Following initial examination, Mrs. T was hospitalized for approximately 4 days. Although she described her recovery following discharge from the hospital as relatively rapid, she continued to complain of decreased visual memory, some visual neglect of the left visual field, fatigue, decreased productivity, and mild word-finding difficulties.

Along with the cognitive deficits noted above, Mrs. T's

profile on the Personality Assessment Profile suggests that she continues to have significant depressive symptoms and somatic concerns and holds onto the belief that she has greatly reduced physical functioning and health.

Collectively, the results of formal assessment and interview converge on the issue of diminished functional, vocational, and personal competence. These concerns are heightened by Mrs. T's thoughts about her own potential return to work. Mrs. T had been viewed by superiors and coworkers as an exceptionally talented and competent manager. In turn, she had taken a great deal of satisfaction and esteem from her status in her work setting. Although Mrs. T wished to return to work, which she greatly valued, the prospect of returning to such an environment at a level of competency that was merely adequate was threatening to her. Clarifying these concerns was critical in developing a rehabilitation and psychotherapeutic plan for Mrs. T. Psychotherapeutically, one focus became increasing her quality of life in the productivity realm, by assisting her in becoming more inclusive in what she viewed as productive (e.g., taking care of her family, recreational pursuits, intellectual pursuits that are not work related).

In addition, an attempt was made to help Mrs. T become more active within the community, as she had become quite isolated following her hospitalization. Her concerns about returning to work prematurely when her stamina and ability continue to be compromised were partially addressed through a work-hardening program. A number of cognitive considerations were critical in working with Mrs. T psychotherapeutically. First, she was trained in the use of a memory notebook. Although she displayed only moderate declines in verbal memory, she did benefit from reviewing daily schedules of appointments, important dates, and "to do" lists. Most important, the notebook was customized to deal with her more severe visual memory problems by including maps of buildings she uses frequently as well as verbal descriptions of local routes she takes often. The therapist also assisted her in compensating for poorer visual memory by teaching strategies in which she could encode visual material (e.g., a map showing directions to a neighboring town) verbally in the form of written directions. Left with very strong verbal comprehension abilities, Mrs. T was a good candidate for bibliotherapy and seemed to enjoy reading information about strategies to assist with vocational re-entry. However, because of visual neglect, the therapist worked with her to draw a red line on the left margin of book pages so that she would consistently find this landmark prior to beginning to read the next line of text. Her mild word-finding difficulties were addressed by assuring Mrs. T that she had ample time to finish her statements in session and allowing her to use gestural cues in her communication with the therapist. Ultimately Mrs. T returned to work part time, which allowed time to prepare for the following day's work and get caught up "off line" and not under the scrutiny of coworkers and superiors. Within 18 months, Mrs. T had made a very successful return to full-time employment in the same job she had previously occupied.

Therapeutic Settings

Group psychotherapy. The potential benefit of group treatment for individuals who have sustained brain injuries is multifaceted. First, the group setting, by nature, addresses psychosocial deficits. These are perhaps the most common deficits following brain injury because personality symptoms of brain injury (e.g., social inappropriateness, impulsivity, sexual changes, increased aggression) so seriously affect social roles and relationships with others. Second, residual impairments that most substantially affect a client's return to vocational or social roles are interpersonal in character and, thereby, well addressed by group psychotherapy. Third, a group structure provides critical peer support and decreased feelings of isolation in the face of fractured social relationships. Finally, the group setting provides an arena for practicing social interaction skills and role playing.

Goals of group therapy. Goals of traditional group therapy, as put forth by Yalom (1985), focus on developing and promoting interpersonal relationships and cohesiveness within the group. In addition, patients in a group setting may be expected to acquire psychoeducational content, follow rules for interacting within the group, or achieve collective insights to be generalized later in more natural contexts. Because of neuropsychological deficits that accompany brain damage, these goals and expectations may be difficult to realize. Langenbahn, Sherr, Simon, and Hanig (1999) suggested that the initial focus of group psychotherapy with clients who have brain injuries should be to rebuild basic underlying social skills as much as possible. This step is followed by practice in the management of emotional reactions to varying reductions in ego defense and cognitive capacities. Structuring techniques, such as giving additional instructions, modeling appropriate responses, cueing frequently, and providing members with a written agenda for the session or a list of ground rules for the group experience, help group members successfully participate in group interaction and generalize experiences from the group setting to their daily lives. Group formats useful for working with brain-injured adults are the psychosocial group, the self-regulation group, and the psychoeducation/support group.

Psychosocial groups attempt to increase client competency in basic living skills, awareness of personal strengths and weaknesses, functional cognitive capacities necessary for staying on task, skills to deliver and use productive feedback from others, basic social interaction, and current psychological and social challenges. Because many issues experienced by brain-injured individuals are universal, these groups often involve a psychoeducation component as well. Treatment strategies include role-playing exercises, topical presentations, structured discussions, and group projects.

Running group sessions. Congruent with any form of therapeutic work with neuropsychologically impaired clients, initial psychosocial group sessions are devoted to fully familiarizing members with the purpose, goals, format, and rules of the group. Subsequent sessions maintain a relatively unchanging format that encompasses segments such as announcements from group members, review of the previous session, introduction of and rationale for the current session, presentation of the topic or engagement in a relevant psychosocial exercise or discussion, and summary of the session.

Videotaping sessions is standard procedure for several reasons. Recordings allow the therapist to develop an understanding of the group's composite personality and can serve as outcome measures. They can be used to demonstrate to a client the impact of his or her behavior on another group member or the group as a whole. Also, recordings can help a member or the group as a whole recall content or the nature of group process from previous sessions and synthesize a holistic perspective on the group experience. In lieu of, or in addition to, videotaping the session the issue of recall can be facilitated by group members' completion of written summaries of each session and keeping of those summaries in their treatment notebooks.

Self-regulation groups. Self-regulation groups help clients emotionally or behaviorally self-regulate. Whereas the psychosocial group deals with broad thematic issues of adjustment and social reintegration following neurological insult, the self-regulation group targets deficits in emotional regulation, impulse control, and self-awareness. Schefft, Malec, Lehr, and Kanfer (1997) suggested that impairments following brain injury can bring about distress, lead to behavioral disability, interfere with self-regulation directly or with attempts to improve self-regulation, and interfere with social support and adjustment.

Goals of the self-regulation group include increasing awareness of self-regulatory difficulties (e.g., the origin of such breakdowns, situations of greatest risk), increasing use of existing strategies for managing emotional processes and teaching new coping or compensatory strategies for self-regulation, and providing group role-play opportunities for practicing effective self-regulatory strategies.

Self-regulation groups work best as time-limited arrangements (i.e., 10–12 weeks in duration) that comprise 1.5- to 2-hr sessions, each focusing on a specific topic with a well-structured agenda. Session content falls into three domains. In the first type of session, group members describe their emotional or behavioral breakdowns, and the group generates viable methods for avoiding similar difficulties in the future. The second type of session centers around hypothetical high-risk scenarios, with group members acting as the "cast of characters." The third type of session has group members practice cognitive-oriented exercises to improve the orientation, attentional, impulse-control, and problem-solving aspects of self-regulation.

Education as intervention. In many cases, the most critical early intervention is education (Bennett, 1987), which is best delivered in psychoeducation/support groups. Patients and their families often feel that health care professionals did not provide enough information about status or prognosis during the acute phases of injury and recovery. Indeed, medical staff members may not supply certain information to avoid further confusing or stressing the patient and family or because busy clinical schedules do not allow enough time for more complete explanations. Also, attempts at explanation can be derailed by the patient's or family's level of distress.

General psychologists can do much to clarify the nature of injuries, acute medical procedures that have taken place, and test findings and to provide the family with information and support. Prigatano and Klonoff (1988) suggested that a psychoeducational model helps the patient and family understand the meaning of brain injury in their lives. Clinicians should explain the mechanism of injury or illness and neuropathologic consequences and take the patient and family chronologically through the recovery course, explaining medical events or intervention in ways they can understand. Most important, the practitioner should formulate an integrated perspective of the patient's neurological, physical, neuropsychological, and psychological status in a noncondescending yet understandable manner. Providing the patient with this information can alleviate a lack of awareness surrounding his or her deficits. Such lack of awareness can be the product of neuropsychological decline or a fundamental psychological defense, such as denial.

It is often easier for the client with a brain injury to receive feedback, including criticism, from other cognitively compromised patients, as is the case in psychoeducation/support groups, than from a clinician. Along with such resistance or denial, another topic for discussion is: Why did this have to happen? The issue of guilt is central to this question. Patients who led high-risk lives prior to the traumatically induced injury often feel they are being punished for previous transgressions. They also may feel anger and a sense that the individuals responsible for the accident should be punished. Prigatano and Klonoff (1988) stated that patients require assistance to achieve self-acceptance and forgiveness of self or others who caused the injury. Other topics for discussion include setting realistic goals, reconceptualizing relationships with family and friends, and learning to advocate for oneself in society at large.

Family intervention. The physical, neurocognitive, behavioral, and emotional impact of a neurological injury or illness can have devastating repercussions not only for the patient but also for the entire family system. Beneficial effects of family involvement in psychotherapy are empirically supported (Rosenthal & Geckler, 1997).

A clinician should assess several components to determine the nature and severity of family difficulty and to intervene with the disruption of the family. Interviewing the family gives the clinician a greater appreciation for family relationships as they existed before the client's head injury; the family's understanding of and perspective on the client's current level of functioning; the family's available financial, emotional, and social resources; and the family's level of insight and subsequent motivation for family intervention. The family can complete more formal, objective assessment tools as well. Two productive methods for evaluating the impact of acquired brain injury on a family are the Family Needs Questionnaire, developed by Kreutzer (1988), and the Head Injury Family Interview, developed by Kay, Cavallo, Ezrachi, and Vavagiakis (1995). The Family Needs Questionnaire provides evidence of a family's need for further medical information or additional emotional or professional support. The Head Injury Family Interview is a structured interview that focuses on premorbid information related to the patient and the family and assesses the significance of the injury on each family member. Both measures have acceptable psychometric characteristics.

Many contexts exist for providing families with the information, insight, and support they require. Depending on issues faced by a family, the family might be best assisted by a family education group, family psychotherapy, supportive family counseling (delivered by a professional), or a community-based family support group (organized by peers).

Topics addressed in family education groups usually include

□ nature of the neurological damage or injury;
□ neurobehavioral consequences most commonly seen with the particular neurological insult;
□ nature of the recovery process;
□ overview of the rehabilitative process, including information regarding roles played by various rehabilitation professionals; and
□ vocational and community re-entry, with specific regard to common obstacles, the role of family in facilitating re-entry, and vocational rehabilitation professionals.

Family psychotherapy allows families to address more specific issues in safe and structured environments with therapists who have been specifically trained to help families struggling with issues that frequently follow neurological illness of a family member. Padrone (1994) suggested that the following factors be considered prior to initiating family therapy: manner in which therapy will be initiated, severity of the patient's disability, issues surrounding the onset of the injury or illness, patient's current stage of rehabilitation, family members' relationships to the patient, patient's life stage, how the patient views his or her disability, nature and dynamics of pre-existing family relationships, and potential sources of countertransference.

Given these variables, specific topical discussions in family therapy are unique to individual families. However, Lezak (1986) outlined the following issues that should be covered:

- ☐ Feelings of anger, frustration, and sorrow are common and should be expected.
- ☐ Family members and other caregivers should not minimize or ignore their own needs and distress.
- ☐ Family members and other caregivers should rely on their consciences and judgment to deal with conflicts.
- ☐ Changing roles within the family are likely to distress everyone and should be expected.
- ☐ Rather than feel guilty for doing too little, family members should realize that doing too much can lead to negative consequences and so should weigh all aspects of a situation.
- ☐ If the welfare of dependent children is at stake, conflict arising from divided loyalties should be acknowledged, and responsibilities should be prioritized.

Even otherwise-healthy families often require support and assistance to deal with the sense of loss, isolation, guilt, and hopelessness that follow neurological impairment of a family member. In supportive family counseling or a family support group, families can interact with other families facing similar challenges. The support provided by such experiences is invaluable, particularly during the early period of adjustment to a family member's disability.

Psychotherapeutic Issues With Other Neurological Populations

Although much attention is given to the psychotherapeutic challenges faced by traumatically brain-injured individuals, less clinical attention is given to other neurological etiologies that have equally dramatic psychosocial consequences. Disorders resulting from CVA or brain tumor produce unique profiles of cognitive deficits and can lead to unique emotional, behavioral, and existential concerns for patients and families.

The focal nature of neuropathology following stroke can lead to affective changes related to cortical involvement or a reaction to decreased functional capacity or autonomy. Left-hemisphere strokes may lead to depressive symptomology or what has been termed the *catastrophic reaction*. Conversely, right-hemisphere loci are more often accompanied by a lack of awareness of ensuing deficits or a casual disregard for the significance of any disability. The focal nature of cerebrovascular events can lead to scenarios in which a number of cognitive functions that allow continued insight are spared. This produces relatively stronger grief and loss reactions than those seen immediately following TBI.

The advanced age of onset in individuals with cerebrovascular disorders also leads to unique psychological issues that involve fear of diminished independence or concerns for family burdened with providing care. Understandably, resentment surfaces as the client watches his or her long-awaited retirement or "golden years" negated.

Tumors involving the central nervous system also present distinct challenges for the patient. In addition to pain, distress, and symptomology brought on by the disease, many clients have to deal with the cognitive decline, discomfort, and fatigue brought on by chemotherapy and radiation. Tumor patients may be left with a sense of uncertainty and dread regarding the potential for recurrence or development of additional cancers. Such concerns can reduce a client's motivation or investment in psychotherapeutic efforts, as he or she may view the future and survival with skepticism.

Conclusion

Although some psychological interventions used with individuals with cognitive impairment are similar to those used with non-neurologically involved psychotherapeutic clients, other strategies may require significant modification or reformulation. Along with directly addressing cognitive deficits that affect functional outcome, the general clinician may find it necessary to alter the pace, focus, or expectations of the psychotherapeutic process to accommodate the unique cognitive capacities of the client with neuropsychological compromise. A solid understanding of comorbid conditions (e.g., substance abuse following TBI) is also critical in preparing to treat the client who has neuropsychological deficits.

Bolstered by the information provided in this book, general clinicians should feel comfortable tapping the resources of allied professionals and referring clients for neuropsychological consultation. He or she should have an increased understanding of basic functional anatomy, common neurological conditions that can affect clinical presentation, and the impact of non-neurological elements on cognitive functioning. The reader also should be better equipped to recognize indicators of neuropsychological impairment and use feedback from the neuropsychological consultation.

Additional Reading

Principles of Neuropsychological Rehabilitation (Prigatano, 1999) provides theoretical and practical coverage of the challenges that exist for the clinician working with clients following brain injury. Ample information is given about cognitive and psychological changes that accompany brain trauma. *Psychotherapeutic Interventions for Adults With Brain Injury or Stroke: A Clinician's Treatment Resource* (Langer, Laatsch, & Lewis, 1999) places primary emphasis on psychotherapeutic interventions with traumatically brain-injured clients and those who have had strokes.

Appendix A

Allied Professional Contact Information

American Academy of Neurology (AAN)
1080 Montreal Avenue
St. Paul, MN 55116

**American Academy of Physical Medicine and
  Rehabilitation (AAPM&R)**
One IBM Plaza, Suite 2500
Chicago, IL 60611

American Occupational Therapy Association (AOTA)
4720 Montgomery Lane
P.O. Box 31220
Bethesda, MD 20824-1200

American Physical Therapy Association (APTA)
1111 North Fairfax Street
Alexandria, VA 22314-1488

American Psychiatric Association (APA)
400 K Street, NW
Washington, DC 20005

American Speech–Language–Hearing Association (ASHA)
10801 Rockville Pike
Rockville, MD 20852

International Neuropsychological Society (INS)
700 Ackerman Road, Suite 550
Columbus, OH 43202

National Academy of Neuropsychology (NAN)
2121 South Oneida Street, Suite 550
Denver, CO 80224-2594

National Association of Social Workers (NASW)
750 First Street, NE, Suite 700
Washington, DC 20002-4241

National Therapeutic Recreation Society (NTRS)
22377 Belmont Ridge Road
Ashburn, VA 20148

Appendix B

Neuropsychological History and Record Review Summary

A. Demographics

Client Name ———————————— Age ——— Date of Birth ————

Education ——— Sex ——— Race/Ethnicity ———— Marital Status ———

Client Address ———————————————————————

———————————————————————

Client Phone ——— Contact Person ———————— Phone ———

Handedness (circle one):   Left   Right   Ambidextrous

Date of Evaluation ————————

B. Presenting Complaints

———————————————————————————

———————————————————————————

———————————————————————————

———————————————————————————

———————————————————————————

C. History of Specific Neurological Events

_____ Head injury   _____ Diagnosis of dementia

_____ Loss of consciousness   _____ Central nervous system tumor

_____ Epilepsy or seizure   _____ Falls

_____ Stroke   _____ Meningitis or encephalitis

_____ Other conditions _____

D. History of Symptoms With Potential Neurological Significance

_____ Dizziness   _____ Headaches (describe)

                                     _____

_____ Fainting   _____ Light-headedness

_____ Weakness in the extremities   _____ Episodes of visual changes or

_____ Tremors   loss

                                     _____ Hearing loss or changes

_____ Numbness   _____ Smell or taste

_____ Other sensory or motor changes _____

_____ Other neurological symptoms _____

E. Previous Neurological Procedures and Findings

_____ CT scan

_____ MRI

_____ EEG

_____ Lab findings

_____ Neurological examination

_____ Other procedures (describe) _____

Findings:

_____

_____

_____

F. Cognitive Changes

Language deficits:

_____ Word-finding _____ Verbal comprehension

Attentional deficits:

_____ Task maintenance _____ Distractibility _____ Impulsivity

Memory deficits:

_____ Name retrieval _____ Recall of recent personal events

Visuospatial deficits:

_____ Visual perception _____ Spatial orientation

Cognitive speed deficits: _____

Problem-solving and reasoning deficits: _____

Description (describe the nature of any problem noted above):

_____

_____

G. Psychosocial Changes

Affective:

_____ Changes in mood _____ Depression _____ Anxiety _____ Stress level

_____ Irritability _____ Energy level _____ Obsessing/worrying _____ Anger

_____ Other (describe) _____

Behaviors:

_____ Sleep habits _____ Sexual functioning _____ Eating _____ Movement

_____ Other (describe) _____

Social:

_____ Relationship with spouse _____ Relationship with parents

_____ Relationship with children _____ Relationship with significant other

_____ Social activities _____ Work relationships _____ Activities at home

Description (describe the nature of any problem noted above):

_____

_____

H. Significant Medical History

Previous surgeries/hospitalizations _____

_____

_____

Serious conditions/illnesses _____

_____

_____

Family medical history _____

_____

_____

Specific conditions:

_____ Heart disease   _____ Thyroid disorder

_____ Hypertension   _____ Lung disease

_____ Cancer   _____ Stomach problems

_____ Anemia   _____ Liver disease

_____ Exposure to toxins   _____ Allergies/asthma

_____ Bone or joint disease   _____ Alcohol/drugs (note) _____

_____ Diabetes

_____ Other conditions (describe) _____

_____

Medications:

Trade/Generic Name	Daily Dose	Date Started	Purpose
_____	_____	_____	_____
_____	_____	_____	_____
_____	_____	_____	_____
_____	_____	_____	_____

I.   Birth/Developmental History

Substances/medications patient's mother had during pregnancy _____

Illness or disease during mother's pregnancy with and delivery of patient:

_____ Natural childbirth	_____ Induced labor
_____ Breech delivery	_____ Respiratory problems at birth
_____ Cesarean	_____ Abnormal color at birth
_____ Forceps used	_____ Slow to cry
_____ Premature or low birthweight (note) _____	_____ Baby was not normally active

_____ Other problems _____

Patient's development:

_____ Age (in months) patient sat up alone

_____ Age (in months) patient crawled

_____ Age (in months) patient walked

_____ Age (in months) patient talked

_____ Problems with toileting

_____ Difficulty getting along with other children

_____ Acting out

_____ Other physical, cognitive, or behavioral problems prior to beginning school

Description (describe the nature of any problem noted above):

_____

_____

J.   Educational and Social History

GPA (estimated/actual) ____ Number of failed grades ____ Which years ____

Best classes/subjects _____ Worst classes/subjects _____

Was patient ever placed in special classes? _____

Did patient ever receive tutoring or counseling at school? _____

Did patient ever avoid or "skip" school? _____

Was patient ever told he or she had a learning disability or specific

problems with math or reading? _____

K. Other Important Personal Incidents

Prior legal involvement _____

_____

_____

Current legal involvement _____

Lawsuit pending _____ no _____ yes (describe) _____

_____

_____

Other notable issues/events _____

Clinician's notes:

_____

_____

_____

_____

Note. CT = computerized tomography; MRI = magnetic resonance imaging;
EEG = electroencephalograph; GPA = grade point average.

Appendix C

Neuropsychological Referral Form

Client Name ⎯⎯⎯⎯ Medical ID Number ⎯⎯⎯ Education ⎯⎯

Date of Birth ⎯⎯ Age ⎯⎯ Sex ⎯ Marital Status S ⎯ M ⎯ D ⎯ W ⎯

Handedness ⎯⎯

Vocational Status ⎯⎯⎯⎯⎯⎯⎯⎯⎯⎯⎯⎯⎯⎯⎯⎯

Home Address ⎯⎯⎯⎯⎯⎯⎯⎯⎯⎯⎯⎯⎯⎯⎯⎯

Referring Clinician/Telephone # ⎯⎯⎯⎯⎯⎯⎯⎯⎯⎯⎯

Etiology ⎯⎯⎯⎯⎯⎯⎯⎯ Loss of consciousness (circle): Yes/No

Reason for Referral for Neuropsychological Services

A. Diagnosis/differential diagnosis questions to be addressed:

⎯⎯⎯⎯⎯⎯⎯⎯⎯⎯⎯⎯⎯⎯⎯⎯⎯⎯⎯⎯⎯

⎯⎯⎯⎯⎯⎯⎯⎯⎯⎯⎯⎯⎯⎯⎯⎯⎯⎯⎯⎯⎯

⎯⎯⎯⎯⎯⎯⎯⎯⎯⎯⎯⎯⎯⎯⎯⎯⎯⎯⎯⎯⎯

⎯⎯⎯⎯⎯⎯⎯⎯⎯⎯⎯⎯⎯⎯⎯⎯⎯⎯⎯⎯⎯

⎯⎯⎯⎯⎯⎯⎯⎯⎯⎯⎯⎯⎯⎯⎯⎯⎯⎯⎯⎯⎯

B. Questions regarding client's cognitive/functional status and potential:

_____

_____

_____

_____

_____

C. Recommendations for providing psychological or rehabilitation
    services to the client:

_____

_____

_____

_____

_____

Client's Presenting Psychological or Cognitive Symptoms

_____

_____

_____

_____

Recent Psychological Test Scores

    Full Scale IQ _____ Verbal IQ _____ Nonverbal IQ _____

    Name of Test _____

Achievement Test Results (standard scores)

    Reading _____ Math _____ Written Expression _____ Spelling _____

    Other (_____) _____

Summary of Objective or Projective Personality Testing

_____

_____

_____

_____

_____

Other Recent Cognitive or Neuropsychological Testing Results

_____

_____

_____

_____

_____

Note. S = single; M = married; D = divorced; W = widowed.

Appendix D

Quality of Life Rating Scale

QUALITY OF LIFE RATING

Client Number _____   Date _____

Quality of Life is related to our values, desires and beliefs, plus our perception of ourselves and our world. Use the key scale statements below to estimate your present quality of life on the 19 factors listed. Give your first impression as you briefly consider each item.

5 = Quality is excellent: no improvement is necessary
4 = Quality is very good: better than I expected
3 = Quality is satisfactory: average compared with my expectations
2 = Quality is not too good: I would like to plan changes
1 = Quality is extremely poor: I need to make changes as soon as possible

Circle one number only

1. Recreation activities 5 4 3 2 1

2. Social/friendly relationships 5 4 3 2 1

3. Close/intimate relationships 5 4 3 2 1

4. Hobbies 5 4 3 2 1

5. Spiritual activities/belief in meaning of life ... 5 4 3 2 1

6. Volunteer activities 5 4 3 2 1

7. Financial conditions 5 4 3 2 1

8. Learning/education/training activities 5 4 3 2 1

9. Work/career activity 5 4 3 2 1

10. Emotional balance 5 4 3 2 1

11. Transportation availability 5 4 3 2 1

12. Sexual adjustment/relationship 5 4 3 2 1

13. Family involvement and support 5 4 3 2 1

14. My physical/bodily condition 5 4 3 2 1

15. Liking/loving of myself 5 4 3 2 1

16. Housing/living conditions 5 4 3 2 1

17. Receiving affection 5 4 3 2 1

18. Control of my life and my future 5 4 3 2 1

19. Amount of stress/tension/pressure
    (5 = no stress; 1 = severe stress) 5 4 3 2 1

20. Overall, I view my life quality as 5 4 3 2 1

Appendix E

Contact Information for Supportive Resources

Alzheimer's Association
National Headquarters
919 North Michigan Avenue
Chicago, IL 60611-1676
1-800-272-3900

American Brain Tumor Association
2770 River Road
Des Plaines, IL 60018
847-827-9910

American Parkinson's Disease Association
1250 Hylan Boulevard, Suite 4B
Staten Island, NY 10305-1946
1-800-223-2732

Brain Injury Association, Inc.
105 North Alfred Street
Alexandria, VA 22314
703-236-6000

Epilepsy Foundation
4351 Garden City Drive
Landover, MD 20785
1-800-332-1000

National Stroke Association
96 Inverness Drive East, Suite I
Englewood, CO 80112-5112
303-649-9299

References

Acker, M. B., & Davis, J. R. (1989). Psychology test scores associated with late outcome in head injury. *Neuropsychology, 3,* 1–10.

Adams, R. D., & Victor, M. (1993). Epilepsy and other seizure disorders. In R. D. Adams & M. Victor (Eds.), *Principles of neurology* (5th ed., pp. 273–299). New York: McGraw-Hill.

Albert, M. S., & Moss, M. D. (1988). *Geriatric neuropsychology.* New York: Guilford Press.

Alexander, M. P. (1987). The role of neurobehavioral syndromes in the rehabilitation and outcome of closed head injury. In H. L. Levin, J. Grafman, & H. M. Eisenberg (Eds.), *Neurobehavioral recovery from head injury* (pp. 191–205). New York: Oxford University Press.

Allen, J. B., Huebner, R. A., Inman, T., Turpin, S., & Gust, T. (1997, November). *Psychometric and normative data on the quality of life rating in physically healthy as well as general medical rehabilitation patients.* Poster presented at the 17th annual meeting of National Academy of Neuropsychology, Las Vegas, Nevada.

Alterman, A. I., & Tarter, R. E. (1985). Assessing the influence of confounding subject variables in neuropsychological research in alcoholism and related disorders. *International Journal of Neuroscience, 26,* 75–84.

Altura, B. M., & Altura, B. T. (1984). Alcohol, the cerebral circulation and strokes. *Alcohol, 1,* 325–331.

American Psychiatric Association. (1994). *Diagnostic and statistical manual of mental disorders* (4th ed.). Washington, DC: Author.

American Psychological Association. (1992). Ethical principles of psychologists and code of conduct. *American Psychologist, 47,* 1597–1611.

Anderson, V. E., & Hauser, W. A. (1993). Genetics. In J. Laidlaw, A. Richens, & D. Chadwick (Eds.), *A textbook of epilepsy* (4th ed., pp. 47–75). Edinburgh, Scotland: Churchill Livingstone.

Artzy, G. (1995). *Correction factors for the MMPI–2 in head injured men and women.* Unpublished doctoral dissertation, University of Victoria, Victoria, British Columbia, Canada.

Baddeley, A. D. (1986). *Working memory.* Oxford, England: Clarendon Press.

Barkley, R. A., Grodzinsky, G., & DuPaul, G. J. (1992). Frontal lobe functions in attention-deficit disorder with and without hyperactivity: A review and research report. *Journal of Abnormal Child Psychology, 20,* 163–188.

Barona, A., Reynolds, C. R., & Chastain, R. (1984). A demographically based index of pre-morbid intelligence for the WAIS–R. *Journal of Consulting and Clinical Psychology, 52,* 885–887.

Barsky, A. J., & Klerman, G. L. (1983). Overview: Hypochondriasis, bodily complaints, and somatic styles. *American Journal of Psychiatry, 140,* 273–283.

Bartell, S. S., & Solanto, M. V. (1995). Usefulness of the Rorschach inkblot test in assessment of attention deficit hyperactivity disorder. *Perceptual and Motor Skills, 80,* 531–541.

Batchelor, E. S., & Dean, R. S. (1996). *Pediatric neuropsychology: Interfacing assessment and treatment for rehabilitation.* New York: Allyn & Bacon.

Bauer, R. M. (1994). The flexible battery approach to neuropsychological assessment. In R. D. Vanderploeg (Ed.), *A guide to neuropsychological practice* (pp. 259–290). Hillsdale, NJ: Erlbaum.

Bennett, T. L. (1987). Neuropsychological counseling of the adult with minor head injury. *Cognitive Rehabilitation, 5*(1), 10–16.

Bennett, T. L. (1989). Individual psychotherapy and minor head injury. *Cognitive Rehabilitation, 7*(5), 20–25.

Berg, R. A., Franzen, M., & Wedding, D. (1994). *Screening for brain impairment: A manual for mental health practice.* New York: Springer.

Bigler, E. D., & Ehrfurth, J. W. (1980). Critical limitations of the Bender–Gestalt test in clinical neuropsychology. *Clinical Neuropsychology, 2,* 88–90.

Billingslea, F. Y. (1963). The Bender-Gestalt: A review and a perspective. *Psychological Bulletin, 60,* 233–251.

Binder, L. M., & Rattok, J. (1989). Assessment of the post-concussive syndrome after mild head injury. In M. D. Lezak (Ed.), *Assessment of the behavioral consequences of head injury* (pp. 37–48). New York: Lisse.

Blair, J. R., & Spreen, O. (1989). Predicting pre-morbid IQ: A revision of the National Adult Reading Test. *The Clinical Neuropsychologist, 3,* 121–136.

Boll, T. J. (1981). The Halstead–Reitan neuropsychological battery. In S. B. Filskov & T. J. Boll (Eds.), *Handbook of clinical neuropsychology* (pp. 577–607). New York: Wiley-Interscience.

Bond, M. R. (1975). Assessment of the psychosocial outcome after severe head injury. In *Outcome of severe damage to the central nervous system* (Ciba Foundation Symposium No. 34, pp. 141–157). Amsterdam: Elsevier-Excerpta Medica.

Bond, M. R. (1984). The psychiatry of closed head injury. In N. Brooks (Ed.), *Closed head injury: Psychological, social and family consequences* (pp. 148–178). New York: Oxford University Press.

Bracy, O. (1994). *Soft tools for cognitive rehabilitation.* Indianapolis, IN: Neuroscience.

Brodal, A. (1981). *Neurological anatomy* (3rd ed.). New York: Oxford University Press.

Brodmann, K. (1909). *Vergleichende Lokalisationlehr der Grosshirnrinde in ihren Prinzipen dargestellt auf Grund des Zellenbaues* [Comparative localization in the cerebral cortex]. Leipzig, Germany: J. A. Barth.

Brooks, N. (1984). Head injury and the family. In N. Brooks (Ed.), *Closed *head injury: Psychological, social, and family consequences* (pp. 123–147). New York: Oxford University Press.

Brooks, N. (1992). Psychosocial assessment after traumatic brain injury. *Scandinavian Journal of Rehabilitation Medicine, 26,* 126–131.

Brown, S., Betts, T., Chadwick, D., Hall, B., Shorvon, S., & Wallace, S. (1993). An epilepsy needs document. *Seizure, 2,* 91–103.

Butcher, J. N., & Harlow, T. (1987). Personality assessment in personal injury cases. In A. Hess & I. Weiner (Eds.), *Handbook of forensic psychology* (pp. 128–154). New York: Wiley.

Butters, N. (1985). Alcoholic Korsakoff's Syndrome: Some unresolved issues concerning etiology, neuropathology, and cognitive deficits. *Journal of Clinical and Experimental Neuropsychology, 7,* 181–210.

Butters, N., & Albert, M. S. (1982). Processes underlying failures to recall remote events. In L. S. Cermak (Ed.), *Human memory and amnesia.* Hillsdale, NJ: Erlbaum.

Butters, N., & Cermak, L. S. (1980). *Alcoholic Korsakoff's syndrome.* San Diego, CA: Academic Press.

Butters, N., & Stuss, D. T. (1989). Diencephalic amnesia. In F. Boller & J. Grafman (Eds.), *Handbook of neuropsychology* (Vol. 3, pp. 107–148). Amsterdam: Elsevier.

Caine, E. D. (1986). The neuropsychology of depression: The pseudodementia syndrome. In I. Grant & K. M. Adams (Eds.), *Neuropsychological assessment of psychiatric disorders* (pp. 221–243). New York: Oxford University Press.

Canter, A. (1976). *The Canter background interference procedure for the Bender–Gestalt test: Manual for administration, scoring, and interpretation.* Los Angeles: Western Psychological Services.

Carberry, H. (1983). Psychological methods for helping the angry, resistant, and negative patient. *Cognitive Rehabilitation, 1*(4), 4–5.

Cassens, G., Wolfe, L., & Zola, M. (1990). The neuropsychology of depressions. *Journal of Neuropsychiatry and Clinical Neurosciences, 2,* 202–213.

Chalfant, J. C. (1984). *Identifying learning disabled students: Guidelines for decision-making.* Burlington, VT: Northeast Regional Resource Center.

Chalfant, J. C. (1989). Learning disabilities: Policy issues and promising approaches. *American Psychologist, 44,* 392–398.

Chelune, G. J., Ferguson, W., Koon, R., & Dickey, T. (1986). Frontal lobe disinhibition in attention deficit disorder. *Child Psychiatry and Human Development, 16,* 221–234.

Chelune, G., Ferguson, W., & Moehle, K. (1986). The role of standard cognitive and personality tests in neuropsychological assessment. In T. Incagnoli, G. Goldstein, & C. Golden (Eds.), *Clinical application of neuropsychological test batteries.* New York: Plenum.

Christensen, A. (1979). *Luria's neuropsychological investigation* (2nd ed.). Copenhagen: Munksgaard.

Cimino, C. R. (1994). Principles of neuropsychological interpretation. In

R. D. Vanderploeg (Ed.), *Clinician's guide to neuropsychological assessment* (pp. 69–112). Hillsdale, NJ: Erlbaum.

Cleaveland, B. L., & Denier, C. A. (1998). Recommendations for health care professionals to improve compliance and treatment outcome among patients with cognitive deficits. *Issues in Mental Health Nursing, 19*, 113–124.

Cohen, R. F., & Mapou, R. L. (1988). Neuropsychological assessment for treatment planning: A hypothesis-testing approach. *Journal of Head Trauma Rehabilitation, 3*, 12–23.

Colantonio, A., Kasl, S. V., Ostfeld, A. M., & Berkman, L. F. (1993). Psychosocial predictors of stroke outcomes in an elderly population. *Journal of Gerontology, 48*, S261-S268.

Constantinidis, J. (1985). Pick dementia: Anatomoclinical correlations and pathophysiological considerations. *Interdisciplinary Topics in Gerontology, 19*, 72.

Corrigan, S. K., & Berry, D. T. R. (1991). Prediction of IQ in normal older persons: A comparison of two methods. *Archives of Clinical Neuropsychology, 17*, 323–324.

Cowan, L. D., Bodensteider, J. B., Leviton, A., & Doherty, L. (1989). Prevalence of the epilepsies in children and adolescents. *Epilepsia, 30*, 94–106.

Crawford, J. R., Parker, D. M., & McKinlay, W. (1992). *A handbook of neuropsychological assessment.* London: Erlbaum.

Crosson, B. A. (1992). *Subcortical functions in language and memory.* New York: Guilford Press.

Crosson, B. A., & Warren, R. L. (1982). Use of the Luria–Nebraska Neuropsychological Battery in aphasia: A conceptual critique. *Journal of Consulting and Clinical Psychology, 50*, 22–31.

Culbertson, J. L., & Edmonds, J. E. (1996). Learning disabilities. In R. L. Adams, O. A. Parsons, J. L. Culbertson, & S. J. Nixon (Eds.), *Neuropsychology for clinical practice* (pp. 331–408). Washington DC: American Psychological Association.

Cummings, J. L. (1985). *Clinical neuropsychiatry.* Orlando, FL: Grune & Stratton.

Cummings, J. L. (1993). Frontal subcortical circuits and human behavior. *Archives of Neurology, 50*, 873–880.

Debettignles, B. H., Swihart, A. A., Green, L. A., & Pirozzolo, F. J. (1997). The neuropsychology of normal aging and dementia: An introduction. In A. M. Horton, D. Wedding, & J. Webster (Eds.), *The neuropsychology handbook (Vol. 2): Treatment issues and special populations* (pp. 173–210). New York: Springer.

Denckla, M. B. (1991). Attention deficit hyperactivity disorder: Residual type. *Journal of Child Neurology, 6*(Suppl.), S44-S50.

Dodrill, C. B. (1978). A neuropsychological battery for epilepsy. *Epilepsia, 27*(Suppl. 2), S64-S76.

Dodrill, C. B. (1979). Sex differences on the Halstead–Reitan Neuropsychological Battery and other neuropsychological measures. *Journal of Clinical Psychology, 35,* 236–241.

Dooneief, G., Mirabello, E., Bell, K., Marder, K., Stern, V., & Mayeux, R. (1992). An estimate of the incidence of depression in idiopathic Parkinson's disease. *Archives of Neurology, 49,* 305–307.

Eames, P. (1988). Behavior disorders after severe head injury: Their nature and causes and strategies for management. *Journal of Head Trauma Rehabilitation, 3,* 1–6.

Evans, D. A. (1990). Estimated prevalence of Alzheimer's disease in the United States. *Milbank Quarterly, 68,* 267–289.

Exner, J. E., Colligan, S. C., Boll, T. J., & Stircher, B. (1996). Rorschach findings concerning closed head injury patients. *Assessment, 3,* 317–326.

Filley, C. M. (1995). *Neurobehavioral anatomy.* Niwot: University Press of Colorado.

Finlayson, M. A. J., & Bird, D. R. (1991). Psychopathology and neuro-psychological deficit. In H. O. Doerr & A. S. Carlin (Eds.), *Forensic neuropsychology: Legal and scientific bases* (pp. 123–140). New York: Guilford Press.

Fischer, D. G., Sweet, J. J., & Pfaelzer-Smith, E. A. (1986). Influence of depression on repeated neuropsychological testing. *International Journal of Clinical Neuropsychology, 8,* 14–18.

Flaskerud, J. H. (1992). Psychosocial and neuropsychiatric care. *Critical Care Nursing Clinics of North America, 4,* 411–420.

Flores, P. J. (1988). *Group psychotherapy with addicted populations.* New York: Haworth.

Ford, C. V. (1983). *The somatizing disorders.* New York: Elsevier.

Franken, E. A., Bergaum, K. S., Dunn, B., Smith, W. L., Ehrhardt, J. C., Levitz, G. S., & Breckenridge, R. E. (1986). Impact of MR imaging on clinical diagnosis and management: A prospective study. *Radiology, 161,* 377–380.

Franzen, M. D. (1989). *Reliability and validity in neuropsychological assessment.* New York: Plenum.

Franzen, M. D., & Berg, R. A. (1998). *Screening children for brain impairment* (2nd ed.). New York: Springer.

Freed, P. (1997). Psychosomatic symptoms following postconcussional syndrome. In J. S. Finell (Ed.), *Mind–body problems: Psychotherapy with psychosomatic disorders* (pp. 311–331). Northdale, NJ: Jason Aronson.

Freud, S. (1957). On narcissism: An introduction. In J. Strachey (Ed. & Trans.), *The standard edition of the complete works of Sigmund Freud* (Vol. 14, pp. 117–140). London: Hogarth Press. (Original work published 1914)

Garske, G. C., & Thomas, K. R. (1992). Self-reported self-esteem and depression: Indexes of psychosocial adjustment following severe traumatic brain injury. *Rehabilitation Counseling Bulletin, 36,* 44–52.

Gerber, P. J., Schnieders, D. A., Paradise, L. V., Reiff, H. B., Ginsberg,

R. J., & Popp, P. A. (1990). Presenting problems of adults with learning disabilities: Self-reported comparisons from their school-age in adult years. *Journal of Learning Disabilities, 23,* 570–573.

Gibb, W. R. (1992). Neuropathology of Parkinson's disease and related syndromes. In J. M. Cedarbaum & S. T. Gancher (Eds.), *Parkinson's disease* (pp. 361–376). Philadelphia: Saunders.

Golden, C. J. (1979). *Clinical interpretation of objective psychological tests.* New York: Grune & Stratton.

Golden, C. J., Hammeke, T. A., & Purisch, A. D. (1982). *The Luria–Nebraska Neuropsychological Battery.* Los Angeles: Western Psychological Services.

Golden, C. J., Purisch, A. D., & Hammeke, T. A. (1985). *Luria–Nebraska Neuropsychological Battery: Forms I and II.* Los Angeles: Western Psychological Services.

Golden, C. J., Sweet, J. J., & Osmon, D. L. (1979). The diagnosis of brain damage by the MMPI: A comprehension evaluation. *Journal of Personality Assessment, 43,* 138–142.

Goldstein, F. C., & Levin, H. S. (1989). Manifestations of personality change after closed head injury. In E. Perecman (Ed.), *Integrating theory and practice in clinical neuropsychology* (pp. 217–243). Hillsdale, NJ: Erlbaum.

Goldstein, K. (1944). The mental changes due to frontal lobe damage. *Journal of Physiology, 17,* 187–208.

Goldstein, K. (1952). The effect of brain damage on the personality. *Psychiatry, 15,* 245–260.

Grant, I., & Adams, K. M. (1996). *Neuropsychological assessment of neuropsychiatric disorders* (2nd ed.). New York : Oxford University Press.

Greenwald, A. G., Pratkanis, A. R., Leippe, M. R., & Baumgardner, M. H. (1986). Under what conditions does theory obstruct research progress. *Psychological Review, 93,* 216–229.

Hachinski, V. (1983). Multi-infarct dementia. In H. J. M. Barnett (Ed.), *Neurology clinics symposium on cerebrovascular disease* (pp. 27–36). Philadelphia: Saunders.

Hall, R., Gardner, E., Stickney, S., LeCann, A., & Popkin, M. (1980). Physical illness manifesting as psychiatric disease II: Analysis of a state hospital inpatient population. *Archives of General Psychiatry, 36,* 414–419.

Hannay, H. J., Bieliauskas, L. A., Crosson, B. A., Hammeke, T. A., Hamsher, K. D., & Koffler, S. P. (1998). Proceedings: The Houston Conference on Specialty Education and Training in Clinical Neuropsychology. *Archives of Clinical Neuropsychology, 13,* 157–250.

Hauser, W. A., & Annegers, J. E. (1993). Epidemiology of epilepsy. In J. Laidlaw, A. Riches, & D. Chadwick (Eds.), *A textbook of epilepsy* (pp. 23–45). Edinburgh, Scotland: Churchill Livingstone.

Heaton, R. R. (1981). *Manual for the Wisconsin Card Sorting Test.* Odessa, FL: Psychological Assessment Resources.

Heaton, R. R., Baade, L. E., & Johnson, K. L. (1978). Neuropsychological test results associated with psychiatric disorders in adults. *Psychological Bulletin, 85,* 141–162.

Heilman, K. M., & Valenstein, E. (Eds.). (1993). *Clinical neuropsychology* (3rd ed.). New York: Oxford University Press.

Hess, A. L., & Hart, R. (1990). The specialty of neuropsychology. *Neuropsychology, 4,* 49–52.

Hesselbrock, M. N., Weidenman, M. A., & Reed, H. B. (1985). Effect of age, sex, drinking history and antisocial personality on neuropsychology of alcoholics. *Journal of Studies on Alcohol, 46,* 313–320.

Hillbom, M., & Holm, L. (1986). Contribution of traumatic head injury to neuropsychological deficits in alcoholism. *Journal of Neurology, Neurosurgery, and Psychiatry, 49,* 1348–1353.

Hirshorn, M. W. (1988, January 20). Freshmen interest in business careers hits new level and money remains a top priority, study finds. *Chronicle of Higher Education,* pp. A31, A34-A36.

Hodges, W. F., & Spielberger, C. D. (1969). Digit span: An indicant of trait or state anxiety? *Journal of Clinical and Consulting Psychology, 33,* 430–434.

Hubel, D. H., & Wiesel, T. N. (1968). Receptive fields and functional architecture of monkey striate cortex. *Journal of Physiology, 195,* 215–243.

Hynd, G. W., & Willis, W. G. (1988). *Pediatric neuropsychology.* Orlando, FL: Grune & Stratton.

Ishii, N., Nishihara, Y., & Imamura, T. (1986). Why do frontal lobe symptoms predominate in vascular dementia with lacunas? *Neurology, 36,* 340.

Jackson, H. F., Hopewell, C. A., Glass, C. A., Warburg, R., Dewey, M., & Ghadiali, E. (1992). The Katz Adjustment Scale: Modification for use with victims of traumatic brain and spinal injury. *Brain Injury, 6,* 109–127.

Jones, B. P., Duncan, C. C., Mirsky, A. F., Post, R. M., & Theodore, W. H. (1994). Neuropsychology profiles in bipolar affective disorder and complex partial seizure disorder. *Neuropsychology, 8,* 55–64.

Joseph, R. (1990). *Neuropsychology, neuropsychiatry, and behavioral neurology.* New York: Plenum.

Jung, R. (1961). Neuronal integration in the visual cortex and its significance for visual information. In W. A. Rosenblith (Ed.), *Sensory communication* (pp. 112–137).

Kamphaus, R. W. (1993). *Clinical assessment of children's intelligence.* Needham Heights, MA: Allyn & Bacon.

Kaplan, E. (1988). A process approach to neuropsychological assessment. In T. Boll & B. K. Bryant (Eds.), *Clinical neuropsychology and brain function: Research, measurement, and practice* (pp. 125–167). Washington, DC: American Psychological Association.

Kaufman, A. S. (1990). *Assessing adolescent and adult intelligence.* Boston: Allyn & Bacon.

Kaufman, A. S., & Lichtenberger, E. O. (1999). *Essentials of the WAIS–III assessment.* New York: Wiley.

Kay, T., Cavallo, M., Ezrachi, O., & Vavagiakis, P. (1995). The Head Injury Family Interview: A clinical and research tool. *Journal of Head Trauma Rehabilitation, 10,* 12–31.

Kelland, D. Z., Bennett, J. M., Mercer, W. N., Caroselli, J. S., & Del Dotto, J. E. (1995). A comparison of MMPI-2 profiles in TBI and non-TBI patients. *Archives of Clinical Neuropsychology, 10,* 349.

Kellner, R., & Sheffield, B. F. (1973). The one-week prevalence of symptoms in neurotic patients and normals. *American Journal of Psychiatry, 130,* 102–105.

Kessler, R. M., Parker, E. S., Clark, C. M., Martin, P. R., George, D. T., Weingartner, H., Sokoloff, L., Ebert, M. H., & Mishkin, M. (1984). Regional cerebral glucose metabolism in patients with alcoholic Korsakoff's syndrome. *Society of Neuroscience Abstracts, 10,* 541.

King, G. D., Caine, E. D., & Cox, C. (1993). Influence of depression and age on selected cognitive functions. *Clinical Neuropsychologist, 7,* 443–453.

Klonoff, P. S., O'Brien, K. P., Prigatano, G. P., Chiapello, D. A., & Cunningham, M. (1989). Cognitive retraining after traumatic brain injury and its role in facilitating awareness. *Journal of Head Trauma Rehabilitation, 4,* 37–45.

Kolb, B., & Whishaw, I. Q. (1996). *Fundamentals of human neuropsychology* (4th ed.). New York: Freeman.

Koran, L. M., Sox, H. C., Marton, K. I., Moltzen, S., Sox, C. H., Kraemer, H. C., Imai, K., Kelsey, T. G., Rose, T. G., & Levin, L. C. (1989). Medical evaluation of psychiatric patients in a state mental health system. *Archives of General Psychiatry, 46,* 733–740.

Kravetz, S. (1973). *Rehabilitation need and status: Substance, structure, and process.* Unpublished doctoral dissertation, University of Wisconsin, Madison.

Kreutzer, J. S. (1988). *Family Needs Questionnaire.* Richmond: Rehabilitation Research and Training Center on Severe Traumatic Brain Injury, Medical College of Virginia.

Laatsch, L. (1996). Benefits of integrating cognitive rehabilitation and psychotherapy in treatment of clients with neuropsychological impairments. *Journal of Cognitive Rehabilitation, 14,* 18–21.

Laatsch, L. (1999). Application of cognitive rehabilitation techniques in psychotherapy. In K. G. Langer, L. Laatsch, & L. Lewis (Eds.), *Psychotherapeutic interventions for adults with brain injury or stroke: A clinician's treatment resource* (pp. 131–148). Madison, CT: Psychosocial Press.

Lachner, G., & Engel, R. (1994). Differentiation of dementia and depression by memory test: A meta-analysis. *Journal of Nervous and Mental Disease*, *182*, 34–39.

Langenbahn, D. M., Sherr, R. L., Simon, D., & Hanig, B. (1999). Group psychotherapy. In K. G. Langer, L. Laatsch, & L. Lewis (Eds.), *Psychotherapeutic interventions for adults with brain injury and stroke: A clinician's treatment resource.* Madison, CT: Psychosocial Press.

Langer, K. G. (1992). Psychotherapy with the neuropsychologically-impaired adult. *American Journal of Psychotherapy, 46,* 620–639.

Langer, K. G. (1999). Awareness and denial in psychotherapy. In K. G. Langer, L. Laatsch, & L. Lewis (Eds.), *Psychotherapeutic interventions for adults with brain injury or stroke: A clinician's treatment resource.* Madison, CT: Psychosocial Press.

Langer, K. G., Laatsch, L., & Lewis, L. (Eds.) (1999). *Psychotherapeutic interventions for adults with brain injury or stroke: A clinican's treatment resource.*Madison, CT: Psychosocial Press.

Langley, M. J. (1995). *Preventing alcohol-related problems after traumatic brain injury: A behavioral approach.* Chicago: Rehabilitation Institute of Chicago.

Lechtenberg, R. (1982). *The psychiatrist's guide to diseases of the nervous system.* New York: Wiley.

Leiner, H. C., Leiner, A. L., & Dow, R. S. (1989). Reappraising the cerebellum: What does the hindbrain contribute to the forebrain? *Behavioral Neuroscience, 103,* 998–1008.

Leli, D. A., & Filskov, S. B. (1984). Clinical detection of intellectual deterioration associated with brain damage. *Journal of Clinical Psychology, 40,* 1435–1441.

Lewis, L., & Langer, K. G. (1994). Symbolization in psychotherapy with patients who are disabled. *American Journal of Psychotherapy, 48,* 231–239.

Lewis, L., & Rosenberg, S. J. (1990). Psychoanalytic psychotherapy with brain-injured adult psychiatric patients. *Journal of Nervous and Mental Disease, 178,* 69–77.

Lezak, M. D. (1983). *Neuropsychological assessment* (2nd ed.). New York: Oxford University Press.

Lezak, M. D. (1986). Psychological implications of traumatic brain injury for the patient's family. *Rehabilitation Psychology, 31,* 241–250.

Lezak, M. D. (1995). *Neuropsychological assessment* (3rd ed.). New York: Oxford University Press.

Lishman, W. A. (1973). The psychiatric sequelae of head injury: A review. *Psychological Medicine, 3,* 304–318.

Lishman, W. A. (1978). *Organic psychiatry: The psychological consequences of cerebral disorder.* London: Blackwell Scientific.

Lishman, W. A. (1987). *Organic psychiatry* (2nd ed.). Oxford: Blackwell Scientific.

Luria, A. (1980). *Higher cortical functions in man.* New York: Basic Books.

Macciocchi, S. N., & Barth, J. T. (1996). The Halstead-Reitan Neuropsychological Test Battery (HRNTB). In C. S. Newmark (Ed.), *Major Psychological Assessment Instruments* (pp.431–459). Boston: Allyn & Bacon.

Malia, K., Powell, G., & Torode, S. (1995). Coping and psychosocial function after brain injury. *Brain Injury, 9,* 607–618.

Malmud, N. (1967). Psychiatric disorders with intracranial tumors of the limbic system. *Archives of Neurology, 17,* 113.

Maloney, M. P., & Ward, M. P. (1976). *Psychological assessment: A conceptual approach.* New York: Oxford University Press.

Margolin, D. I. (1992). Probing the multiple facets of human intelligence: The cognitive neuropsychologist as clinician. In D. I. Margolin (Ed.), *Cognitive neuropsychology in clinical practice.* New York: Oxford University Press.

Margolis, E. T. (1993, August). Individual psychotherapy with the brain-injured adult: A treatment for the soul? In W. R. Leber (Chair), *Psychotherapy for brain-damaged patients.* Symposium conducted at the 101st Annual Convention of the American Psychological Association, Toronto, Ontario, Canada.

Martin, G. N. (1998). *Human neuropsychology.* Hemel Hempstead Hertfordshire, England: Prentice Hall Europe.

Maruish, M. E., Sawicki, R. F., Franzen, M. D., & Golden, C. J. (1985). Alpha coefficient reliabilities for the Luria-Nebraska Neuropsychological Battery Summary and localization scales by diagnostic category. *International Journal of Clinical Neuropsychology, 7,* 10–12.

Maslow, A. H. (1970). *Motivation and personality* (2nd ed.). New York: Harper and Row.

Mateer, C. A. (1983). Motor and perceptual functions of the left hemisphere and their interaction. In S. J. Segalowitz (Ed.), *Language functions and brain organization* (pp. 80–110). Orlando, FL: Academic Press.

Mattis, S. (1988). Dementia Rating Scale (DRS). Odessa, FL: Psychological Assessment Resources.

Mattson, A. J., & Levin, H. S. (1990). Frontal lobe dysfunction following closed head injury. *Journal of Nervous and Mental Disease, 178,* 282–291.

Mayes, A. R. (1988). *Human organic memory disorders.* New York: Cambridge University Press.

McKhann, G., Drachman, D., Folstein, M., Katzman, R., Price, D., & Stadlan, E. M. (1984). Clinical diagnosis of Alzheimer's disease. *Neurology, 34,* 939–944.

McKinlay, W. W., & Brooks, D. N. (1984). Methodological problems in assessing psychosocial recovery following severe head injury. *Journal of Clinical Neuropsychology, 6,* 87–99.

McLean, A., Jr., Dikmen, S., Temkin, N., Wyler A. R., & Gale, J. L. (1984). Psychosocial functioning at one month after head injury. *Neurosurgery, 14,* 393–399.

Meehl, P. E. (1954). *Clinical versus statistical prediction.* Minneapolis: University of Minnesota Press.

Mesulam, M.-M. (2000). *Principles of behavioral and cognitive neurology* (2nd ed.). New York: Oxford University Press.

Milberg, W. P., Hebben, N. A., & Kaplan, E. (1986). The Boston process approach to neuropsychological assessment. In I. Grant & K. Adams (Eds.), *Neuropsychological assessment of neuropsychiatric disorders*, New York: Oxford University Press.

Miller, L. (1987). Neuropsychology of the aggressive psychopath: An integrative review. *Aggressive Behavior, 13*, 119–140.

Miller, L. (1991). Brain and self: Toward a neuropsychodynamic model of ego autonomy and personality. *Journal of the American Academy of Psychoanalysis, 19*, 213–234.

Miller, L. (1993). *Psychotherapy of the brain-injured patient: Reclaiming the shattered self*. New York: Norton.

Miller, L. (1997). Freud and consciousness: The first one hundred years of neuropsychodynamics in theory and clinical practice. *Seminars in Neurology, 17*, 171–177.

Millon, T., Green, C., & Meagher, R. (1979). The MBHI: A new inventory for the psychodiagnostician in medical settings. *Professional Psychology, 10*, 529–539.

Millon, T., Green, C., & Meagher, R. (1982). Millon Behavioral Health Inventory manual (3rd ed.). Minneapolis, MN: National Computer Systems.

Mirra, S. S., Heyman, A., McKeel, D., Sumi, S. M., Crain, B. J., Brownlee, L. M., Vogel, F. S., Hughes, J. P., van Belle, G., Berg, L., & participating CERAD neuropathologists. (1991). The Consortium to Establish a Registry for Alzheimer's disease (CERAD). Part II. Standardization of the neuropathologic assessment of Alzheimer's disease. *Neurology, 41*, 479–486.

Mitrushina, M. N., Boone, K. B., & D'Elia, L. F. (1999). *Handbook of normative data for neuropsychological assessment*. New York: Oxford University Press.

Mittenberg, W., DiGiulio, D. V., Perrin, S., & Bass, A. E. (1992). Symptoms following mild head injury: Expectation as aetiology. *Journal of Neurology, Neurosurgery, and Psychiatry, 55*, 200–204.

Morey, L. (1991). *Personality Assessment Inventory: Professional manual*. Odessa, FL: Psychological Assessment Resources.

Murray, H. A. (1971). *Thematic Apperception Test: Manual*. Cambridge, MA: Harvard University Press. (Original work published 1943)

Moses, Jr., J. A., & Purisch, A. D. (1997). The evolution of the luria-Nebraska neuropsychological battery. In G. Goldstein & I. Incagnoli (Eds.), *Contemporary approaches to neuropsychological assessment* (pp. 131–170). New York: Plenum Press.

National Head Injury Foundation. (1988). *National Head Injury Foundation/ Professional Council Substance Abuse Task Force white paper*. Southborough, MA: Author.

Neary, D., & Snowden, J. S. (1991). Dementia of the frontal type. In H. S.

Levin, H. M. Eisenberg, & A. L. Benton (Eds.), *Frontal lobe function and dysfunction*. New York: Oxford University Press.

Nelson, H. E., & O'Connell, A. (1978). Dementia: The estimation of premorbid intelligence levels using the new adult reading test. *Cortex, 14*, 234–244.

Oades, R. D. (1987). Attention deficit disorder with hyperactivity (ADDH): The contribution of catecholamine activity. *Progress in Neurobiology, 29*, 365–391.

Oberholzer, E. (1931). On differential diagnosis of psychological sequelae after head trauma by means of the Rorschach from interpretation experiment. *Zeitschrift für die Gesamte Neurologie und Psychiatrie, 136*, 596–629.

O'Hara, C. (1988). Emotional adjustment following minor head injury. *Cognitive Rehabilitation, 6*(2), 26–33.

Olanow, C. W. (1992). Magnetic resonance imaging in Parkinson's disease. *Neurology Clinics, 10*, 405–420.

Padrone, F. J. (1994). Psychotherapeutic issues with family members of persons with physical disabilities. *American Journal of Psychotherapy, 48*, 195–207.

Palmer, J. (1985). Advances in imaging technology and their applications. *Medical Journal of Australia, 142*, 3–4.

Paolo, A. M., Troster, A. I., Glatt, S. L., Hubble, J. P., & Koller, W. C. (1994, February). *Utility of the Dementia Rating Scale to differentiate the dementias of Alzheimer's and Parkinson's Disease*. Paper presented to the International Neuropsychological Society, Cincinnati, OH.

Pasino, J. (1979). Factors influencing management and outcome: Psychological considerations. In Professional Staff Association of Rancho Los Amigos Hospital (Eds.), *Rehabilitation of the head-injured adult: Comprehensive physical management*. Los Angeles: Editor.

Passingham, R. E. (1987). From where does the motor cortex get its instructions? In S. P. Wise (Ed.), *Higher brain functions* (pp. 67–97). New York: Wiley.

Perry, W., Potterat, E., Auslander, L., & Kaplan, E. (1996). A neuropsychological approach to the Rorschach in patients with dementia of the Alzheimer's type. *Assessment, 3*, 351–363.

Piotrowski, Z. (1937). The Rorschach inkblot method in organic disturbances of the central nervous system. *Journal of Nervous and Mental Diseases, 86*, 525–537.

Plassman, B. L., Havlik, R. J., Steffens, D. C., Helms, M. J., Newman, T. N., Drosdick, D., Phillips, C., Gau, B. A., Welsh-Bohmer, K. A., Burke, J. R., Guralnik, J. M., & Breitner, J. C. S. (2000). Documented head injury in early adulthood and risk of Alzheimer's disease and other dementias. *Neurology, 55*, 1158–1166.

Pope, H. G. J., Gruber, A. J., & Yurgelun-Todd, D. (1995). The residual neuropsychological effects of cannabis: The current status of research. *Drug and Alcohol Dependence, 38*, 25–34.

Prendergast, M., & Binder, D. (1975). Relationships of selected self-concept and academic measures. *Measurement and Evaluation in Guidance, 8,* 92–95.

Prigatano, G. P. (1987). Personality and psychosocial consequences after brain injury. In M. J. Meier, A. L. Benton, & L. Diller (Eds.), *Neuropsychological rehabilitation* (pp. 355–378). New York: Churchill Livingstone.

Prigatano, G. P. (1999). *Principles of neuropsychological rehabilitation.* New York: Oxford.

Prigatano, G. P., Amin, K., & Rosenstein, L. D. (1993). Validity studies on the BNI screen for higher cerebral functions. *BNI Quarterly, 9,* 2–9.

Prigatano, G. P., & Klonoff, P. S. (1988). Psychotherapy and neuropsychological assessment after brain injury. *Journal of Head Trauma Rehabilitation, 3,* 45–56.

Psychological Assessment Resources. (1983). *Neuropsychological Status Examination (NSE).* Odessa, FL: Psychological Assessment Resources.

Psychological Corporation. (1992). *Wechsler Individual Achievement Test.* San Antonio, TX: Author.

Purisch, A. D., & Sbordone, R. J. (1986). The Luria–Nebraska Neuropsychological Battery. In G. Goldstein & R. E. Tarter (Eds.), *Advances in clinical neuropsychology* (Vol. 3, pp. 291–316). New York: Plenum.

Putnam, S. H., & Millis, S. R. (1994). Psychosocial factors in the development and maintenance of chronic somatic and functional symptoms following mild traumatic brain injury. *Advances in Medical Psychotherapy, 7,* 1–22.

Reitan, R. M. (1972). Verbal problem-solving as related to cerebral damage. *Perceptual and Motor Skills, 34,* 515–524.

Reitan, R. M. (1986). Theoretical and methodological bases of the Halstead–Reitan neuropsychological test battery. In I. Grant & K. M. Adams (Eds.), *Neuropsychological assessment of neuropsychiatric disorders* (pp. 3–30). New York: Oxford University Press.

Reitan, R. M., & Wolfson, D. (1985). *The Halstead–Reitan Neuropsychological Test Battery.* Tucson, AZ: Neuropsychology Press.

Reitan, R. M., & Wolfson, D. (1992). *Neuroanatomy and neuropathology: A clinical guide for neuropsychologists* (2nd ed.). Tucson, AZ: Neuropsychology Press.

Reitan, R. M., & Wolfson, D. (1993). *The Halstead–Reitan neuropsychological test battery* (2nd ed.). Tucson, AZ: Neuropsychology Press.

Richards, P. M., & Ruff, R. M. (1989). Motivational effects of neuropsychological functioning: Comparison of depressed versus nondepressed individuals. *Journal of Consulting and Clinical Psychology, 57,* 396–402.

Rorschach, H. (1951). *Psychodiagnostics.* New York: Grune & Stratton.

Rosenberg, M. (1965). *Society and the adolescent self image.* Princeton, NJ: University Press.

Rosenthal, M., & Geckler, C. L. (1997). Family intervention in neuropsychology. In A. M. Horton, D. Wedding, & J. Webster (Eds.), *The neuropsychology handbook, Vol. 2: Treatment issues and special populations* (pp. 47–72). New York: Springer.

Rourke, B. P. (1982). Central processing deficiencies in children: Toward a developmental neuropsychological model. *Journal of Clinical Neuropsychology, 4*, 1–18.

Rourke, B. P., Bakker, D. J., Fisk, J. L., & Strang, J. D. (1983). *Child neuropsychology: An introduction to theory, research, and clinical practice*. New York: Guilford Press.

Saling, M. (1994). Report writing in neuropsychology. In S. Touyz, D. Byrne, & A. Gilandas (Eds.), *Neuropsychology in clinical practice* (pp. 394–400). Sydney, Australia: Harcourt Brace.

Saper, C. B. (1990). Hypothalamus. In A. L. Pearlman & R. L. Collings (Eds.), *Neurobiology of disease*. New York: Oxford University Press.

Schefft, B. K., Malec, J. F., Lehr, B. K., & Kanfer, F. H. (1997). The role of self-regulation therapy with the brain-injured patient. In M. E. Maruish & J. A. Moses Jr. (Eds.), *Clinical neuropsychology: Theoretical foundations for practitioners* (pp. 237–282). Mahwah, NJ: Erlbaum.

Schwamm, L. H., VanDyke, C., Kiernan, R. J., Merrin, E. L., & Mueller, J. (1987). The neurobehavioral cognitive status examination. *Annals of Internal Medicine, 107*, 486–491.

Shepherd, G. M. (1988). *Neurobiology* (2nd ed.). New York: Oxford University Press.

Simon, D., Riley, E., Egelko, S., Kaplan, E., Newman, B., & Diller, L. (1991, August). *A new instrument for assessing awareness of deficits in stroke.* Poster presented at the 99th Annual Convention of the American Psychological Association, San Francisco.

Small, L. (1980). *Neuropsychodiagnosis in psychotherapy* (rev. ed.). New York: Brunner/Mazel.

Smokler, I. A., & Shevrin, H. (1979). Cerebral lateralization and personality style. *Archives of General Psychiatry, 36*, 949–954.

Snyder, P. J., & Nussbaum, P. D. (1998). *Clinical neuropsychology: A pocket handbook for assessment*. Washington, DC: American Psychological Association.

Sohlberg, M. M., & Mateer, C. A. (1989). *Introduction to cognitive rehabilitation: Theory and practice*. New York: Guildford Press.

Soukup, V. M., & Adams, R. L. (1996). Parkinson's disease. In R. L. Adams, O. A. Parsons, J. L. Culbertson, & S. J. Nixon (Eds.), *Neurology for clinical practice: Etiology, assessment, and treatment of common neurological disorders*. Washington, DC: American Psychological Association.

Sox, H. C., Jr., Blatt, M. A., Higgins, M. C., & Morton, K. I. (1988). *Medical decision making*. Boston: Butterworths.

Sparadeo, F. R., & Gill, D. (1989). Effects of prior alcohol use on head injury recovery. *Journal of Head Trauma Rehabilitation, 4*, 75–81.

Speedie, L. J., Rabins, P. V., & Pearlson, G. D. (1990). Confrontation naming deficit in dementia of depression. *Journal of Neuropsychiatry and Clinical Neurosciences, 2,* 59–63.

Spilker, B. (1990). *Quality of life in clinical trials.* New York: Raven Press.

Spreen, O., & Strauss, E. (1998). *A compendium of neuropsychological tests: Administration, norms, and commentary.* New York: Oxford University Press.

Stagle, D. A. (1990). Psychiatric disorders following CHI: An overview of biopsychosocial factors in their etiology and management. *International Journal of Psychiatry in Medicine, 20,* 1–35.

Stevenson, J. M., & King, J. H. (1987). Neuropsychiatric aspects of epilepsy and epileptic seizures. In R. E. Hales & S. C. Yudofsky (Eds.), *Textbook of neuropsychiatry* (pp. 209–224). Washington, DC: American Psychiatric Press.

Stroop, J. (1935). Studies of interference in serial verbal reactions. *Journal of Experimental Psychology, 18,* 643–661

Strub, R. L., & Black, F. W. (1988). *Neurobehavioral disorders: A clinical approach.* Philadelphia: Davis.

Sweet, J. J., Moberg, P., & Westergaard, C. (1996). Five-year follow-up survey of practices and beliefs of clinical neuropsychologists. *Clinical Neuropsychologist, 10,* 202–221.

Sweet, J. J., & Westergaard, C. (1997). Psychopathology and neuropsychological assessment. In G. Goldstein & T. M. Incagnoli (Eds.), *Contemporary approaches to neuropsychological assessment* (pp. 325–358). New York: Plenum.

Taylor, R. L. (1990). *Mind or body: Distinguishing psychological from organic disorders.* New York: Springer.

Teeter, P. A., & Semrud-Clikeman, M. (1997). *Child neuropsychology: Assessment and interventions for neurodevelopmental disorders.* New York: Allyn & Bacon.

Tramontana, M. G., & Hooper, S. R. (1988). Child neuropsychological assessment: Overview of current status. In M. G. Tramontana & S. R. Hooper (Eds.), *Assessment issues in child neuropsychology: Critical issues in neuropsychology* (pp. 3–38). New York: Plenum.

Vanderploeg, R. D. (Ed.). (2000). *Clinician's guide to neuropsychological assessment* (2nd ed.). Mahwah, NJ: Lawrence Erlbaum.

Vogt, A. T., & Heaton, R. L. (1977). Comparison of WAIS indices of cerebral dysfunction. *Perceptual and Motor Skills, 45,* 607–615.

Walsh, K. (1994). *Neuropsychology: A clinical approach* (3rd ed.). New York: Churchill Livingstone.

Ward, M. F., Wender, P. H., & Reimherr, F. W. (1993). The Wender Utah Rating Scale: An aid in the retrospective diagnosis of attention deficit hyperactivity disorder. *American Journal of Psychiatry, 150,* 885–890.

Watson, C. G. (1971). An MMPI scale to separate brain-damaged from functional psychiatric patients in neuropsychiatric settings. *Journal of Consulting and Clinical Psychology, 36,* 121–125.

Wechsler, D. (1958). *The measurement and appraisal of adult intelligence* (4th ed.). Baltimore: Williams & Wilkins.

Wechsler, D. (1991). *Wechsler Intelligence Scale for Children–III*. San Antonio, TX: Psychological Corporation.

Wechsler, D. (1997a). *Wechsler Adult Intelligence Scale–III manual*. San Antonio, TX: Psychological Corporation.

Wechsler, D. (1997b). *Wechsler Memory Scale III* (3rd ed.). San Antonio, TX: Psychological Corporation

Wedding, D., & Faust, D. (1989). Clinical judgment and decision making in neuropsychology. *Archives of Clinical Neuropsychology, 4,* 233–265.

Weitzner, M. A., Meyers, C. A., & Byrne, K. (1996). Psychosocial functioning and quality of life in patients with primary brain tumors. *Journal of Neurosurgery, 84,* 29–34.

Wells, C. E. (1979). Pseudodementia. *American Journal of Psychiatry, 136,* 895–900.

Wender, P. H. (1995). *Attention-deficit hyperactivity disorder in adults*. New York: Oxford University Press.

Werner, H. (1937). Process and achievement: A basic problem of education and developmental psychology. *Harvard Educational Review, 7,* 353–368.

White, R. F. (1992). *clinical syndromes in adult neuropsychology: The practitioner's handbook*. Amsterdam, The Netherlands: Elsevier Science.

Whitehead, W. E., Winget, C., Fedoravicius, A. S., Wooley, S., & Blackwell, B. (1981). Learned illness behavior in patients with irritable bowel syndrome and peptic ulcer. *Digestive Diseases and Sciences, 27,* 202–208.

Whitehouse, P. J., Hedreen, J. C., White, C. L., & Price, D. L. (1983). Basal forebrain neurons in dementia of Parkinson's disease. *Annals of Neurology, 13,* 243–248.

Whiteneck, G. G. (1994). Measuring what matters: Key rehabilitation outcomes. *Archives of Physical Medicine and Rehabilitation, 74,* 1073–1076.

Wiederholt, W. C. (1982). Cerebrovascular disease. In W. C. Wiederholt (Ed.), *Neurology for non-neurologists* (pp. 179–189). New York: Academic Press.

Wilkinson, G. S. (1993). *WRAT3 administration manual*. Wilmington, DE: Jastak Associates.

Williams, M. A., & Boll, T. J. (1997). Recent advances in neuropsychological assessment of children. In G. Goldenstein & T. M. Incagnoli (Eds.), *Contemporary approaches to neuropsychological assessment* (pp. 231–276). New York: Plenum.

Williamson, D. J. G., Scott, J. G., & Adams, R. L. (1996). Traumatic brain injury. In R. L. Adams, O. A. Parsons, J. L. Culbertson & S. J. Nixon (Eds.), *Neuropsychology for clinical practice: Etiology, assessment, and treatment of common neurological disorders* (pp. 9–64). Washington, DC: American Psychological Association.

Wolber, G., & Lira, F. T. (1981). Relationship between Bender designs and basic living skills of geriatric patients. *Perceptual and Motor Skills, 52,* 16–18.

Wolf, J. K. (1980). *Practical clinical neurology.* Garden City, NY: Medical Examination Publishing.

Wolfson, D. (1985). *Neuropsychological history questionnaire.* Tucson, AZ: Neuropsychology Press.

Woodcock, R. W. (1998). *The WJ-R and Batería in neuropsychological assessment: Research report Number 1.* Itasca, IL: Riverside.

Woodcock, R. W., & Johnson, M. B. (1989). *Woodcock-Johnson Psychoeducational Battery-Revised.* Chicago: Riverside Publishing.

World Health Organization Quality of Life Group. (1996). The World Health Organization Quality of Life Assessment (WHOQOL): Position paper from the World Health Organization. *Social Science and Medicine, 41,* 1403–1409.

Yalom, I. D. (1985). *The theory and practice of group psychotherapy* (3rd ed.). New York: Basic Books.

Zangwill, O. L. (1966). Psychological deficits associated with frontal lobe lesions. *International Journal of Neurology, 5,* 395–402.

Author Index

Subject Index

ACA. *See* Anterior cerebral artery
Academic achievement, tests of, 120–121
Acalculia, 44
Acquired immune deficiency syndrome (AIDS), 156
ADHD. *See* Attention deficit/hyperactivity disorder
Affective disorders, 92–93, 100
African Americans, 65
Aggression, 173–174
Aging, 14–15, 65
AIDS (acquired immune deficiency syndrome), 156
Alcohol abuse, 111, 176–180
Alcohol dementia, 177
Alzheimer's disease, 21, 107, 153
   dementia related to, 67–70, 98
   and head trauma, 62
American Neuropsychiatric Association, 21
American Psychological Association, 136
Amygdala, 40
Aneurysms, 64, 66
Anomia, 44
Anosagnosia, 65, 175
Anterior cerebral artery (ACA), 53, 64–66
Anteriovenous malformations, 66
Anxiety disorders, 93
Aphasia, 39, 70
Apraxia, 70, 110
Arachnoid layer, 53
Astrocytes, 51
Atherosclerosis, 64–65
Attention deficit/hyperactivity disorder (ADHD), 87–89
Attention deficits, 167
Awareness difficulties, 175–176
Axon hillock, 33, 35

Axons, 33–35, 46

Barona formula, 149
Barrow Neurological Institute Screen (BNIS), 126–127
Basal ganglia, 39–40
Basilar nucleus of Meynert, 73
Bender—Gestalt test, 119–120, 122
BNIS. *See* Barrow Neurological Institute Screen
Boston Process Approach, 145–146
Bradyphrenia, 74
Brain, 34–51
   cerebral cortex of, 40–49
   in children, 13
   development of, 46–47
   subcortex of, 38–40
   theories of brain function, 49–51
   tumors in, 76–79
Brain abcesses, 80
Brain injury. *See* Traumatic brain injury
Brain stem, 29, 34–38
Brodmann's areas, 46

Case management, 164
Catastrophic reaction, 191
Caudate, 40
Central nervous system (CNS), 16, 29, 102. *See also* Brain
   and glucose, 82
   neoplasms of, 77
   and reflexes, 17
Cerebellum, 36, 38–39
Cerebral aqueduct, 36
Cerebral arteries, 53, 56
Cerebral cortex, 29, 40–49
   frontal lobe of, 45–46
   left/right hemisphere of, 41
   occipital lobe of, 41, 43–44
   organization of, 40–42

233

About the Author

Jeffery B. Allen, PhD, ABPP-ABCN, is associate professor at the School of Professional Psychology at Wright State University in Dayton, Ohio. He has served as postdoctoral fellow at the Rehabilitation Institute of Michigan in Detroit and has been a clinical neuropsychologist for Cardinal Hill Rehabilitation Hospital in Lexington, Kentucky. He is widely published in the fields of neuropsychology, head injuries, and memory, and his work has appeared in such journals as *Neuropsychologica, Brain Injuries,* and *Archives of Clinical Neuropsychology and Assessment.* Dr. Allen is a diplomate in clinical neuropsychology. His areas of teaching include physiological psychology and clinical neuropsychology. Among his interests are neurobehavioral disorders, quality of life in medical populations, cognitive and neuropsychological assessment, and outcome measurement in rehabilitation. In 2000, Dr. Allen was elected fellow in the National Academy of Neuropsychology.